READERS LOVE THIS BOOK

"In this aching, honest, and moving account of coming to terms with his son's Asperger diagnosis, Ron Fournier speaks to every parent who has struggled with not only accepting but embracing his or her child's differences. Quite frankly, that is every one of us. To varying degrees we all have two children; the one we hoped for and the one we have. It is the latter that is the blessing. Love That Boy reminds us not to be preoccupied with weaknesses but to look for strengths. Ultimately, Fournier sees clearly, without projection or intruding narcissism, the gift that he has been given in his quirky, whip-smart, and unforgettable son Ty. A brave and beautiful recounting."

—MADELINE LEVINE, PH.D., AUTHOR OF *THE PRICE OF PRIVILEGE* AND *TEACH YOUR CHILDREN WELL*

"This illuminating and touching book gives us the great gift of letting us know and appreciate the Asperger's world of young Tyler Fournier, who steals scenes from presidents while teaching his parents and all of us what is important in life."

—DAVID MARANISS, PULITZER PRIZE-WINNING AUTHOR OF *ONCE IN A GREAT CITY: A DETROIT STORY*

"Ron Fournier has done a masterful job capturing the troubles and triumphs of parenting. That we—as parents and caring adults—too often superimpose our own needs and aspirations on the children we love is an important theme in this must-read new book. It is a moving tale of fatherhood and of coming to terms with a more enlightened definition of perfect."

—STEPHEN GRAY WALLACE, PRESIDENT AND DIRECTOR OF THE CENTER FOR ADOLESCENT RESEARCH AND EDUCATION (CARE)

"There's no magic wand that can make the challenges of parenting disappear, but having the courage to talk honestly about them may be the next best thing. This is a candid look at raising an atypical child. Ron Fournier leads by example, digging through expectations and ego to lay bare what it means to love a child unconditionally."

—OLIVIA MORGAN, MANAGING EDITOR, *THE SHRIVER REPORT*; MEMBER OF THE BOARD, NEW ENGLAND CENTER FOR CHILDREN

"Ron Fournier's deeply personal account of the frustrations and celebrations that go along with raising a special child is deeply moving. As the proud father of an Asperger's child, Ron's heartfelt work inspired me as much as I know it will inspire you."

—JOE SCARBOROUGH, NBC NEWS SENIOR POLITICAL ANALYST AND HOST OF *MORNING JOE*

"American presidents have the honor of meeting Tyler Fournier in this lovely, intimate, and inspiring book by his father, which has so much to teach all parents, sons, and daughters."

—MICHAEL BESCHLOSS

"Love That Boy *captures both the fears and gifts of fatherhood and writes about it with honest, selfless clarity. This book is a joy to read and should be required for all new dads . . . Really.*"

—JIM GAFFIGAN, COMEDIAN AND AUTHOR OF *DAD IS FAT*

"Ron Fournier and his son Tyler are partners on an eye-opening road trip to the crossroads of love and humanity. Along the way, they meet Bill Clinton and George Bush; but the real reward for readers from his being on the road with his dad is that we meet Tyler, a young man with Asperger's and a heart as big as the country."

—MIKE BARNICLE, JOURNALIST AND MSNBC NEWS ANALYST

LOVE THAT BOY

What Two Presidents, Eight Road Trips,
and My Son Taught Me About
a Parent's Expectations

RON FOURNIER

HARMONY
BOOKS · NEW YORK

Copyright © 2016 by Ron Fournier
Reader's Guide copyright © 2017 by Penguin Random House LLC.

All rights reserved.
Published in the United States by Harmony Books, an imprint
of the Crown Publishing Group, a division of Penguin Random
House LLC, New York.
crownpublishing.com

Harmony Books is a registered trademark, and the Circle colophon
is a trademark of Penguin Random House LLC.

This work is adapted from "First, Family," as originally published in
National Journal magazine, on December 1, 2012.

Originally published in hardcover in the United States by Harmony
Books, an imprint of the Crown Publishing Group, a division of
Penguin Random House LLC, New York, in 2016.

Library of Congress Cataloging-in-Publication Data is available
upon request.

ISBN 978-0-8041-4050-8
Ebook ISBN 978-0-8041-4049-2

Printed in the United States of America

Cover design by Jessie Sayward Bright
Cover photographs: (front) Gallery Stock; (spine) Shutterstock/
Robert Cicchetti

10 9 8 7 6 5 4 3 2 1

First Paperback Edition

To mothers and fathers, and to their children who are
greater than any dream, especially:

Ron and Flo

Holly, Gabrielle, and Tyler

Above all, Lori

CONTENTS

INTRODUCTION

Washington, D.C.—*Our noses almost touched the wall. Tall, white, and seamless, it was the only thing standing between us and the president of the United States. "Stay right there," a White House aide told my wife and three children. "The president will be with you in a minute." Suddenly the wall opened; it was a hidden door to the Oval Office. "Come on in, Fournier!" shouted George W. Bush from behind his desk. "Who ya dragging in?"*

It was my last day covering the White House for the Associated Press, and this April 2003 visit was a courtesy that presidents traditionally afford departing correspondents. I introduced my wife, Lori, and two daughters, Holly and Gabrielle, before turning to their younger brother, 5-year-old Tyler.

"Where's Barney?" my son shouted.

The five of us stood in front of Bush's desk, which, like everything else about the Oval Office, had a history. One of the most famous pictures of the Kennedy era, taken a few weeks before the president's assassination, captured John F. Kennedy Jr. playing at his father's feet beneath the same desk, which the younger JFK considered to be his secret clubhouse.

Behind Bush, outside broad southern windows, sat a tiny black dog—its back to the Oval Office and its eyes fixed on the street beyond the White House fence.

Getting up to shake hands, the president blocked Tyler's view of the windows. "Where's Barney?" Tyler shouted again, in a voice so inappropriately loud and demanding that I jumped slightly.

Bush smiled and nodded—first to an aide and then to the lawn. "He's coming. He's right there. He likes to sit out there."

Tyler launched into a one-sided conversation, firing off one choppy phrase after another with machine-gun delivery. "Scottish terriers are called scotties, they originated from Scotland, they can be traced back to a single female named Splinter II, President Roosevelt had one, he called it Fala. Dad says he kept him in the office down there when he was swimming, there's one in Monopoly, my favorite is the car . . ."

Tyler stopped when the Scottish terrier scampered into the room and started sniffing the guests. "Watch out!" Bush laughed. "He's a guard dog."

"Barney!" Tyler yelled. "Barney!"

I cringed. Tyler was a loving, charming, and brilliant boy—he had a photographic memory—but he was somehow different. His voice was jarringly deep and loud for a kid his age. He fixated on topics, like presidential history and animals. He was, in a word, quirky. But the president was enchanted. He laughed, listened, and asked Tyler several questions about dogs before gathering us together for photos.

"Look at your shoes," Bush told Tyler while putting a hand on my boy's shoulder and steering him toward the photographer. "They're ugly. Just like your dad's." Tyler's head rocked back in laughter, and his right foot kicked out; his whole body shook.

A few minutes later we were walking out of the Oval Office when Bush grabbed me by the elbow. "Love that boy," he said, holding my eyes. I thought I understood what he meant. I didn't.

It took me years to understand.

A PARENT'S LOVE is unconditional. A parent's satisfaction comes with caveats. This is an important distinction: You *love* your kids no matter what, but you *expect* them to be something—smart or popular or successful, maybe a scholarship athlete who marries well and runs the family business.

These expectations often are older than the kids they define. I know a couple in Maryland who decorated their unborn daughter's pink room with stencils and statues of ballerinas. A Pennsylvania homemaker tied a string to a bride-and-groom cake topper and hung the faux happy couple from the mobile in her girl's nursery. Big dreams, early pressure—like the Virginia firefighter who put a red light and ladder on his son's crib. "He may not be born yet," the fireman told me, "but I know he's going into his daddy's line of work."

When a woman is pregnant, we say she is expecting. Expecting a baby and filling with expectations. Log on to any mommy website and witness the longing. "At this point, I don't have any concrete expectations on him," a soon-to-be Midwest mother told me at WhatToExpect.com, before contradicting herself in the next keystrokes: "We expect him to be involved with music one way or another since both of us were, and his dad still performs with the local symphonies." Parenthood is a paradox. "We all want the same thing from our kids," the Virginia fireman said, "that perfect boy or girl."

Parenthood is the last chance to be the person we hoped to be. We want to get it right. We want it to be perfect, and that's the problem. It's a hard slog between aspiration and realization. Most of us lurch between the dark and the light, between seething with injustice that Junior and Jane didn't follow the "right" path (ours) or get what they deserve, and chastising ourselves for the demands we make.

On one hand, we know our kids can't be perfect. But we don't accept it. The definition just might apply: "Having all the required or desirable elements, qualities, or characteristics; as good as it is possible to be."

From their first breath—if not sooner—our dreams for our children are at least in the ballpark of perfect, because great grades, championship trophies, lots of friends, and professional success lead to happiness, right?

Actually, no. When a parent's expectations come from the wrong place and are pressed into service of the wrong goals, kids get hurt. I discovered this late in my job as a father.

I AM A journalist who has covered or overseen coverage of the White House and national politics since 1993, an ego-inflating career that I often put ahead of my wife and kids. Lori and I met at the University of Detroit, married a year after graduation, and quickly started our family. Holly was born in 1988, followed by Gabrielle almost four years later, and Tyler five years after that. While Tyler was a bright, funny, and loving boy, he was not exactly what I envisioned in a son: He hated sports, which I loved, and he was socially awkward, which made me uncomfortable.

All good things in my life start with Lori, including the story behind this story. Tyler was 12 years old and I was consumed by the 2010 congressional elections when Lori became hooked on a new NBC drama called *Parenthood*. It featured a large and loving extended family of Bravermans, including a boy named Max who had Asperger's syndrome, a mild form of autism. Max

frequently lost his temper, rarely made friends, and fixated on insects. His parents, Adam and Kristina, rico-
cheted between pride and fear. While they recognized
Max was gifted in his own ways—he was brilliant and
preternaturally genuine—they couldn't escape the fact
that he was a social misfit.

From the first episode, Lori recognized Tyler in
Max—and cried. While our son's issues weren't as
severe as Max's, Lori now realized that Tyler's social
awkwardness was more than a phase. He wasn't just
quirky. His fixations weren't just cute; they were a
clue. His grades had fallen. Classmates teased him. He
had no friends except for boys on the block, who didn't
play with Tyler as much as they tolerated him. Lori
thought, *He's not going to outgrow it.* She watched three
more episodes by herself, not wanting to share her fears
with me, because I might confirm them. Instead, she
kept telling herself, *I don't want him to be autistic.*

Max's parents hired an Asperger's specialist, who
patiently taught the teenager how to start and maintain
conversations, how to feign interest in others' interests,
and why basic hygiene is important. Lori realized Tyler
might benefit from a specialist's help, too. That's when
she told me to watch *Parenthood.* Sitting alone at my
computer until 3:00 a.m., catching up on a half season
of episodes, I saw what Lori saw. I wept with fear. Also
relief: At least now we knew what we were dealing
with.

The first specialist Lori hired was Dr. Mittie T. Quinn, a psychologist specializing in psychoeducational testing, in McLean, Virginia. "Your boy is fascinating for somebody like me," she said. Dr. Quinn sat on a high-backed chair across from her office sofa, where Lori and I nervously held hands. An unfinished puzzle sat on the floor next to a worn wooden train with its locomotive missing. "He's got all kinds of stuff going on. But he's just a charming, charming kid."

I pulled a pen and pad out of my computer bag; 25 years as a reporter in Arkansas and Washington, and I had never been so anxious to record a conversation.

"Attention: His internal motor revs so much faster than normal. . . . I'd hate to see what he's like when he's off the attention-deficit medicine. My heart goes out to him because he's such a bright kid. . . . This makes him impulsive. He can't help but blurt things out. . . . Don't yell at him." (WE YELL!)

"Intelligence: Even with impulse and distraction issues, Tyler is unusually bright. . . . He's a sponge. . . . His IQ measured at 110–120. If we could factor out the attention issues, potentially he'd be far, far above 130." (CAN WE EVER FACTOR OUT?)

"Executive functioning: Handwriting bad . . . Hard time shifting tasks. Timed tasks freak him out. . . . He's a big-picture guy who can figure out the meaning of things by the context. . . . Clumsy movement . . . Severe fine-motor issues." (NO SPORTS?)

"Social/emotional: Spectrum disorder. Twirls hair, flaps his arms . . . Tyler feels for the world. He is empathetic. He loves people but can't easily put himself in people's shoes. . . . Can't pick up social clues, facial clues . . . Can't step outside himself and see how world hears him . . . Tyler fits pretty classically the Asperger's piece." (???)

Looking up from my notes, I asked, "What's Asperger's?"

"High-functioning autism," Dr. Quinn said, "but don't worry."

Don't worry. You just told me my son is autistic, *but don't worry.* You slapped a label on our negligence—all the signs we missed or ignored over the years: clumsy, impulsive, loud, and no social graces—*but don't worry.* Don't yell at him? Yelling is one of my most reliable parenting tools! My mind raced: *What's with the severe motor issues?*

"Does that explain why he's so bad at sports?" I asked.

"Yes," Dr. Quinn said, "and it probably explains why he doesn't like them."

Having turned her diagnosis into a scouting report, I now felt the warm flush of guilt rise in my face. I had entered fatherhood assuming the only way I could connect with Tyler—*the only way I could be a good dad*—was to play sports with him, like my father had with me.

While I focused on my shattered dreams, Lori asked the right question, "So what do we do?"

IF TYLER IS the protagonist of this story, Lori is the hero. It was her idea to send Tyler and me on the road together after his diagnosis. We needed to bond, she said, and Tyler needed real-world experience to learn how to socialize. The trips would augment the training that Tyler would now get in school and through a team of therapists Lori was putting together. She had long since abandoned her career to raise our kids.

One of Tyler's obsessions was history, and my job was covering the U.S. presidency. This made Lori's first decision an easy one. From the moment we walked out of Dr. Quinn's office, she knew the destinations of our trips: the homes and libraries of past presidents— Washington, Adams, Roosevelt, Kennedy, and Ford, for starters. Lori even urged me to try to arrange visits with Barack Obama, Bill Clinton, and George W. Bush. I thought she was joking: *That'll never happen.* But she was dead damn serious, telling me, "You can use a job that took you away from Tyler to help him now."

Lori told me to take notes on the trips. She told me to write a magazine article about them, then this book, so that Tyler would forever remember how much we loved him. But first I had to learn to love my boy for who he was, rather than what I wanted him to be.

The history junkie in me thought I might even learn something about parenting from the founding fathers, most of whom did a lousy job with their children. I admire Tyler's favorite president, Theodore Roosevelt, for the way he struggled to temper his expectations. Writing weekly to each of his absent children, Teddy bared guilt, angst, and love in a passive-aggressive voice you might find familiar. "I am entirely satisfied with your standing, both in your studies and in athletics," Roosevelt wrote his eldest son, Ted junior, on May 7, 1901. "I want you to do well in your sports, and I want even more to have you do well with your books; but I do not expect you to stand first in either, if so to stand could cause you to overwork and hurt your health."

THESE DREAMS WE have for our kids come from many places. The first place is found within every parent. Think back to when you started to seriously consider having kids. Why did you want to be a mom or dad? Did you want to love somebody else, or did you want somebody else to love *you*? Did you want to create a new life, or improve *yours*? Did you want to contribute to a new generation, or did you want to help *shape* one? Cynthia Edwards, a developmental psychologist at Meredith College, in Raleigh, North Carolina, calls these the fundamental questions of parenthood. Most mothers and fathers, if they're being honest with themselves, "discover that they became a parent for a combination of selfless and selfish reasons," she said. "We're all, at some level, compensating."

The original sin of parenting is the baggage we drag into it. Each of us, every mother and father, was once an awkward kid chasing daydreams across the years. Then life interrupted our hunt. None of us is a Disney princess or a superhero. Our families don't resolve their conflicts playfully and prayerfully around a noisy dinner table in exactly 60 minutes. We're not all pro athletes, Ivy League graduates, and Nobel Prize winners. We didn't take over Dad's company or inherit Mom's grace on the gymnastics mat. We're too tall or too short, too fat or too skinny, and more mediocre than we had hoped we'd be. We rush into parenthood just in time to compensate for our shortcomings.

We send out our children not as they are but as we think they should be. And, oh, the props: contact lenses, braces, acne cures, and designer clothes . . . prescription drugs, therapists, beach weeks, and tutors . . . SAT prep, sports trainers, internships, and summers abroad. Some parents hit the DNA jackpot and their kids meet or exceed their wildest dreams. For most of us that doesn't happen. Most of us are average, and we raise average kids. They ride the bench, worship *Star Trek*, develop paunches, or grow hair in odd places. Mothers and fathers don't want to admit they're raising ugly or awkward ducklings. Rather than accepting these gifts—our brilliantly unique children—we reshape them.

I know a mother and father on the West Coast who

never got over their high school A-list envy. They spent thousands of dollars on pictures for their daughter Sandra's senior year, come-hither shots by a professional photographer, and thousands more on a prom dress and senior trip, all despite the fact that the father was out of work and borrowing money from family. After graduation, Sandra lost her motivation, lost contact with her friends, dropped out of college, and forever pined for the past. "She peaked in high school," her aunt told me.

We project so much upon our kids in part because we pour so much into them. Starting in the early 20th century, when a child's role in the family shifted from economic necessity (working on farms and in factories) to economic burden (thanks to laws against child labor), parents looked to their progeny for emotional affirmation. Modern parents fret and sweat and regret over their children to the extent that they become, as Carl Honoré wrote in *Under Pressure*, "an extension of the parental ego—a mini-me to eulogize around the water cooler or on Web sites."

I plead guilty to the mini-me mind-set. Years ago, a colleague reminded me that Take Your Child to Work Day was coming up. "Are you bringing Tyler?" she asked. "I've heard so much about him."

"He can't get out of school," I lied. The truth was, I worried that his social awkwardness would be embarrassing.

THE PRESSURE IS also external. For instance, popular culture is a conveyer belt of expectations. Movies, television, books, magazines, advertisements, and websites—so many websites!—portray parenting as a high-stakes competition for bright, gorgeous, athletic, rich, happy, polite, funny, charismatic kids, packaged and assembled by The Perfect Parents.

If you owned a TV in the last few years, surely you saw Gerber's life insurance ad. It featured several young couples seated around a table, drinking coffee and chatting. "So, has anybody actually started saving for college yet?" one man asks the other couples. Cue parental anxiety about education, personal finances, and the economy. The ad drove me nuts. First, it induced pangs of guilt about the little planning Lori and I had done for our kids' futures. *Hey, honey! Do we have insurance for the kids? College plans? Friends who like coffee?* Second, it angered me, because life as a parent is fretful enough without a multinational company preying on your fears. The ad's subtext is clear: If you bring your newborn home from the hospital without a college fund, you suck as a parent.

The more I thought about the ad—and the millions of messages like it coursing throughout popular culture—the more I saw the trap set for our kids: Outsizing expectations is big business in America. *You're going to college, kid, and it better be a damn good one. We got a Gerber Life College Plan!*

Even when popular culture and commercialization get it right, the scripts put our lives to shame. There's a scene from *Parenthood* in which Max's father explains how he adjusted to the boy's insect fixation. "I wish that he had been more into baseball than bugs. But that's not how it turned out," Adam Braverman told his brother, a new father. "So now I'm into bugs." How many parents watched that scene and asked themselves: *Why can't I be more like Adam?* Other than me, I mean.

There is another major source of parental expectations. Dreaming big is how mothers and fathers seize control from chaos, which is the essential ingredient of parenting these days. An unforgiving global economy and the Great Recession are punishing families, and kids today arguably have the worst economic prospects of any generation in eight decades. Even more, communication technologies expose them to the darkest corners of humanity. The Internet and ubiquitous media hasten children into adulthood with images that glorify sexual promiscuity, violence, commercialism, greed, and vanity.

This is a scary time to raise kids, and with that anxiety comes the temptation to smother our children in expectations. "Contemporary hyper-parenting is a true product of our times," wrote authors Alvin Rosenfeld and Nicole Wise in *The Overscheduled Child*. Edwards, a child development professional and the mother of two young children, said she should know better—and yet she heard "the clock ticking," her ambitions roiling, from the first day of her pregnancy. "It's sort of natural, though damaging, to put enormous pressure on these kids before we send them out into this world," Edwards said, "and to demand perfection almost from day one." Before day one, actually.

Heidi Murkoff's book *What to Expect When You're Expecting* is considered the pregnancy bible, a global blockbuster that, according to her website, spawned a series of books "to help guide parents through pre-conception, pregnancy, parenting, and beyond." Soon-to-be mothers and fathers can register at Murkoff's site and get updates to help track their baby's progress, gain access to message boards where hand-wringing parents trade advice, and receive e-coupons for diapers, vitamins, educational software, and other products appealing to parental palpitations.

If expectations are a trap, whattoexpect.com is honey bait. An interactive graphic on its homepage allows parents to toggle along a timeline from "One Week Pregnant" to "3rd Year" and compare their child's progress to the site's expectations. Underlying each how-to story is an unspoken critique.

- 5 Weeks Pregnant: "How Big Is Your Baby?"
  (Translation: Your baby looks sort of small. Is it okay?)

- 10 Weeks Pregnant: "Ways to Nurture Your Relationship." *(You need to get along better with your kid!)*
- 17 Weeks Pregnant: "What Your Baby Can Do This Week." *(What's your baby not doing? There might be something wrong!)*
- 39 Weeks Pregnant: "Prepping for Childhood." *(Dear Lord, you're not ready to be a mom!)*

The Internet is awash in the business of bearing perfect babies. Ads and ad-supported content nag parents: Play music near the womb (classical, not country), talk to him (soothing tones, adult words), read to her (the classics, ideally), touch the mother's belly and feed her lots of omega-3 fatty acids. One article had 25 tips so contradictory and complicated that my stomach hurt by the time I got to this nugget: "Stay relaxed and stress-free."

Relax. It might help to realize we're not the first generation of parents to raise kids in scary times. To pick a period in history, the late 1800s and early 1900s presented parents with challenges that echo ours. First, wrenching economic change (from a farm-based economy to an industrial one) left millions of workers in the lurch and transformed the family structure. Income inequality grew, social mobility declined, and the public lost faith in a broad array of social and political institutions that previously had buoyed families.

New technologies like the telegraph and automo-

biles were transforming American life while com-
plicating a parent's work. For instance, sociologists
linked increases in teenage pregnancy to the popu
larization of cars (and their ubiquitous rumble seats),
which gave young men and women unprecedented
freedom from parental supervision. New media of
the day—newspapers, magazines, popular books,
radio broadcasts, traveling preachers, salesmen, and
promoters—exposed children to "a continuous barrage
of exotic ideas and projects," according to *Middletown
Families*, a landmark analysis in 20th-century sociol-
ogy. Insatiably in search of new audiences, 19th- and
early-20th-century journalists sensationalized crimes,
such as the random murder of a Chicago boy by Na-
than Leopold and Richard Loeb.

Thanks to scientific and social advances, it was, like
today, the safest and most rewarding time yet in human
history to raise a child. And yet mothers and fathers at
the turn of the 20th century felt anxious and adrift,
certain of only one thing: the world awaiting their kids
would be quite different from their own.

TYLER WAS NOT ready for the world that awaited him,
Dr. Quinn told us the day she diagnosed him. Just 12
years old, he was showing signs already of depression
due to the ostracism experienced by most Aspies. "Life
is getting worse, and worse in a hurry, for him," she
said.

Lori squeezed my hand. I stared at the powerless train and a single puzzle piece lying at my feet—misfits of a tidy office. "He's sad," the doctor continued. "Nobody understands him. Kids make fun of him, and he's left out."

There was good news, Dr. Quinn said. Tyler had found a way to cope. While others might find his constant joking to be off-putting, he was using humor as an outlet. Dr. Quinn giggled. "Do you know what Tyler said when I told him he needed to show more empathy? He gave me a big, confident smile and said, 'I know. I'm working on that.'"

We thanked the doctor, left her office, and walked into the parking lot, where Lori sprang on me her idea for a father-son project. "Now it's time to step up," she said before we got to the car. "Tyler would feel valued if you took the time to take these trips with him." On the drive home, Lori's muffled sobs almost drowned out her grim prediction: "He's going to be so lonely."

Her pleading unearthed a deep wellspring of shame. If I had been home more, would we have diagnosed Tyler sooner? When I was home, did my preoccupation with the job steal attention from my boy? Did the girls also suffer for my ego? Did my marriage take a backseat? And why didn't Tyler already feel valued by his father? Lori is a wise woman. I think she knew it was time I started questioning myself. And so began what I called guilt trips.

Part One

WHAT
WE WANT

NORMAL

"Did I Grow Up According to Plan?"

Washington, D.C.—*We started slow and close to home—five miles away, to be exact—at 1600 Pennsylvania Avenue. Lori wanted our first trip to be at the place where I spent most of my time away from our kids. When the invitation came from the White House for the 2010 media holiday party, Lori handed me the unopened envelope and said, "I'm not going this year. Take Ty."*

That was two weeks ago. Tyler and I are now standing in line at the party, a gold-fringed red carpet beneath our feet and a crystal chandelier above our heads. A tuxedoed waiter offers Tyler a flute of cranberry juice. "Nope," Tyler says. The line inches closer to President Obama and First Lady Michelle Obama, who are posing for pictures with members of the White House press corps, a decades-old tradition meant to ease tensions between reporters and the reported. Critics consider this press party a prime example of Washington's incestuous culture. They're right, but that's not the point of this story. This is about my boy.

A lithe waitress presents Tyler with a tray of bacon-wrapped shrimp. "Uh-uh," he says, turning to a table of cheese and crackers and loudly proclaiming, "Are you kidding me?" Each time he refuses the food, I tell my 13-year-old, "Be polite, son." It's been six months since Tyler was diagnosed with Asperger's syndrome. He doesn't know when he's too loud or when he's talking too much. He can't read facial expressions to tell whether somebody is happy, sad, or bored. He has a difficult time stepping outside of himself to see how he is viewed by others. Was he rude to the waiters or just honest? Tyler doesn't always know the difference. He is what polite company calls "socially awkward" or "a bit off." Bullies call Tyler "weird." Even I don't always know what to make of him.

I'm not just embarrassed about his manners; I'm embarrassed about being embarrassed. After all, this kid would do anything to please me. I expect him to behave; he does. I expect him to respect his mom; he does. I love sports; he hates them, but he plays for me. Guilt and helplessness gnaw at any parent—most deeply for a father like me, whose expectations exceed his common sense, and who for years missed and ignored signs that his child needed help.

Tyler and I inch toward the Green Room, in line with blow-dried TV anchors and stuffy columnists. He's practicing his handshake and hello: "It's a pleasure to meet you, Mr. President. It's a pleasure to meet you, Mr. President. It's a pleasure to meet you, Mr. President." When the couple in front of us steps forward for their picture, my teenager with sky-blue eyes and a soft heart looks up at me and says, "I hope I don't let you down, Dad."

What kind of father raises a son to worry about embarrassing his dad? Worse, how could I be so pathetically unable to help my boy? I want to tell Tyler not to worry, that he'd never let me down. That there's nothing wrong with being different. That I actually am proud of what makes him special. But we are next in line to meet the president of the United States in a room filled with fellow strivers, and all I can think about is the real possibility that Tyler might embarrass himself. Or, God forbid, me.

It is now our turn. The president shakes my hand while Tyler approaches Mrs. Obama. "Still playing hoops?" the president asks me, recalling the pickup game we played during the 2008 presidential campaign. "Yes, sir," I reply as we pose stiffly for pictures. Out of the corner of my eye, I see Mrs. Obama gently brush Tyler's bangs from his eyes and lean in for a hug. I worry for a moment that Tyler will pull away because he's not comfortable with being touched, especially by strangers. But he embraces the First Lady, wishes her a merry Christmas, and then shuffles to his left to look her husband squarely in the eye and shake his hand. "It's a pleasure to meet you, Mr. President." My stomach clenches as I realize the problem here isn't my son. It's not even autism. It's me.

SITTING KNEE TO knee at a coffee shop counter, Stacey Bromberg and I stared self-consciously out a window onto a strip-mall parking lot while she ripped scraps of cardboard from the sleeve of her cup and cried. "I guess you never think of the possibility of something not being—for the lack of a better word—perfect." Bromberg is the mother of two elementary school children, including a son, Gavin, who struggles with attention-deficit disorder and social skills. "It's been hard on the family," she said. "Hard on our marriage."

From a speaker directly above our heads, Louis Armstrong's "What a Wonderful World" gave way to Simple Plan's "Perfect." The mythology of excellence is so pervasive in our culture that its Greek chorus chased me down at a Starbucks. "Did I grow up according to plan?" a young man asks his father in the song. "I'm sorry I can't be perfect."

Stacey ignored the music, blew on her coffee, and continued. "He doesn't fit in at school," she said. I asked how Gavin's issues were hard on her marriage. Nothing major, Stacey replied, "but we don't always agree on what to do for him." Gavin's doctors wanted to sharpen his focus with medication. Stacey fought against them. Her husband, Adam, was more open to drugs. Gavin broke the tie. "I like who I am," the fifth-grader told his parents. "I don't want to change my personality."

WHY DO WE struggle so much over what makes our children different? Despite the fact that all of us are less than average at most things, we don't want our kids flirting with society's Mendoza line. Smaller than normal . . . taller than normal . . . heavier than normal . . . skinnier than normal . . . sicker than normal . . . weaker than normal. For nine months, expectant mothers and fathers worry about childhood deafness, dwarfism, Down syndrome, and various other physical and learning disabilities that could dash their dreams. Sexuality is another bugaboo. Straight parents expect to have straight kids because that's what they know— and because they think being gay in America is harder than being hetero.

The most primal of parental expectations is the desire to see your child accepted, to avoid the dastardly a-words: *atypical* and its caustic cousin, *abnormal*. Lori had an endearing way of expressing this desire. "All I want," she said during each of her three pregnancies, "is a baby with ten fingers and ten toes." In other words, no defects. Stacey and Adam Bromberg would not use the word *defective* to describe Gavin any more than Lori and I would use it to describe Tyler. We love our boys. But let's be honest: When your children aren't anything like you—or like anything you expected—you struggle to understand them, which makes it more difficult to connect with them.

In his bestselling book, *Far from the Tree*, Andrew Solomon analyzes families with children who are disabled, gifted, or otherwise different from what their mothers and fathers expected. Parents, he concludes, must ask themselves this question: Do I simply accept my kids for who they are, or do I push them to become their best selves? Solomon wrote, "My mother didn't want me to be gay because she thought it wouldn't be the happiest course for me, but equally, she didn't like the image of herself as the mother of a gay son."

Her son *is* gay. Solomon's book destroys one of the biggest myths of parenting: A "normal" kid is better off than one who is different. In fact, he argues, we've all got our quirks. "The exceptional is ubiquitous; to be entirely typical is the rare and lonely state," Solomon wrote. "As my parents had misapprehended who I was, so other parents must be constantly misapprehending their own children."

After I wrote a magazine article about my relationship with Tyler, a reader, Russell S., emailed me about his father. "I always wanted to impress him," wrote the public relations executive for a Fortune 500 company. "I thought the only way to get him to like me was to do things he liked. But I don't think I ever lived up to his potential. I was never good in sports—a killer, considering my Bronx-born dad once worked at Yankee Stadium. And I am in my mid-30s with no kids. He'll *never* say it, but I always feel like I cannot give him what he wants. I sometimes think I embarrass him."

I called Russell at his Manhattan office and asked

what exactly he thought his dad wanted from him. "I feel guilty that I'm not giving my dad or any dad what they expect in a son," he replied.

"What's that?" I pressed. Russell was holding something back.

"You expect to become a grandparent," Russell said. "It's almost an unspoken social convention that you give your parents [grandchildren]." He coughed to cover up the teary crack in his voice. "I'm gay."

Russell paused. I sensed that he wanted me to change the subject. Finally he filled the silence. "It's probably not going to happen for me—children," he continued. "I often think, when I die, where's the name going to go? I feel a real responsibility, and I'm not sure it's the right kind of guilt."

I asked how his parents had handled the news. "We've never had the talk," he said. "Of course they know. But I've never had the coming-out talk with them."

The closest Russell's father came to accepting his son's sexuality was during a roundabout conversation one Thanksgiving. "Maybe you'll never have children," his dad said, "but before I leave this earth I want to know that you're being taken care of and being loved."

"Thank you," Russell replied.

In *Far from the Tree*, Solomon also argues that the aversion to raising an "atypical" child is exacerbated in

parents who assume they're raising an echo of themselves. "Parenthood abruptly catapults us into a perma-
nent relationship with a stranger, and the more alien
the stranger, the stronger the whiff of negativity," he
wrote. "We depend on the guarantee in our children's
faces that we will not die. Children whose defining
quality annihilates the fantasy of immortality are a
particular insult; we must love them for themselves,
and not for the best of ourselves in them, and that is a
great deal harder to do."

Looking back, Alan Dworkin knows that was his
mistake. A successful attorney from South Carolina,
Dworkin always wanted a boy whom he could teach to
play sports, and who might follow him into the legal
profession. His son Mitch turned out to be a klutz,
both socially and physically, the kind of boy who had
trouble making friends and avoiding bullies. Dworkin
thought golf would help Mitch meet people and learn
to control his impulses. Bad idea.

Mitch, who was about 8 years old when his dad
first brought him to the golf course, gripped the club
like a baseball bat. "He couldn't play a lick," Alan said.
Worse, while Alan's pals and clients lined up putts,
Mitch chattered and darted to the flag pin. "I'd pull
him back—I wouldn't yell—and I'd whisper in his ear,
'You don't do that when somebody's putting.'" But the
boy had no sense of social propriety. Alan once introduced Mitch to a new client, a woman with a large

mole on her cheek. The boy pointed at the ugly mass and asked her what was wrong with her face. Alan was horrified.

Mitch is now 50. He remembers the pain and shame of embarrassing his father. "I tried to please my dad a lot as a child, but he was kind of hard on me," Mitch said. "I kind of felt just like I couldn't do anything right." Mitch felt the pressure of his dad's expectations until those expectations were reset by a doctor's findings. Mitch was in his 30s when a doctor diagnosed him with anxiety, depression, and obsessive-compulsive disorder, and in his 40s when labeled an Aspie. "Until then," Mitch said, "Dad was not being unreasonable in what he was expecting."

Alan loves Mitch. He has always loved Mitch. But it's only been in the last 15 or so years that Alan has *understood* his son, and with that knowledge comes guilt. "When I think about what I did and didn't do," Alan said, "I just want to cry."

EVEN AS A toddler Tyler was mesmerizing—a handsome, blue-eyed packet of precocious energy, with the vocabulary and curiosity of a college professor and the joyful charisma of a comedian. Everybody in the family has a favorite Tylerism, a story that illustrates his old-soul intelligence and wit.

I remember him in the middle of the night, on

tiptoes from inside his crib, turning on his bedroom light and yelling, "I want to play with *choo* guys!" That huge crinkly-eyed smile. He slept with a heavy blanket pulled over his head, no matter how hot it got, and would pretend to snore with an exaggerated "honk-shee!" While speech and vocabulary came easily to Tyler, conversation did not. He spoke in monologues and on tangents, with an oddly commanding voice. When somebody tried to interrupt him—because it wasn't a good time for a small boy to be talking, or he was totally off topic—Tyler seemed physically incapable of stopping his thought process. He just had to finish, pounding out his thoughts in hurried, quick bursts of speech.

Lori recalls a visit to the mall when Tyler saw a baby boy crying. Rather than quietly asking Lori what was wrong, our preschooler plunged into the other mother's personal space—his nose almost touched her knee—and shouted, "'Cuse me, ma'am. 'Cuse me, ma'am. What's wrong with your son?" On another shopping trip Tyler grew restless as Lori helped Holly pick out a dress for senior prom. Sprawling across the aisle, Tyler declared, "My blood sugar level is dangerously low!"

Holly's favorite Tylerism is listening to her brother try to negotiate his way out of a shower. "When I get free will, I'm not gonna shower every night anymore," Tyler said. "I'll flip a coin. Heads, I shower. Tails, I don't." Most little boys don't like taking showers. Few link the chore with the philosophy of free will. He hated collared shirts—couldn't stand the textured fabric against his neck—and called them "style-cramping shirts."

One of Tyler's first teachers had a strict rule: Any student who forgot his or her pencil needed to give the teacher a shoe as collateral for a loaner. Most kids remembered their pencils most days. But with his attention-deficit disorder and a hyperliteral sensibility, Tyler coped this way: Every morning for an entire school year, he took off his left shoe at his locker (which was filled with pencils, by the way) and limped down the hall to English class. "Here ya go!" he'd tell the teacher, handing her his shoe. "Where's my pencil?"

Before history and social sciences, Tyler's fixation was animals. He stumped zookeepers in Washington with his obsessive, encyclopedic memory. One night the family was playing a trivia game with some friends. Two teams were stuck on a question: What's the world's largest rodent? For laughs, Holly ran to another room and asked her toddler brother the question. Tyler shrugged and said, "Capybara," in a no-brainer tone of voice, as if his sister had asked him the color of the sun.

We didn't recognize the symptoms of high-functioning autism—his pseudo-adult intellect, vocabulary, and baritone; his awkward social interactions and obsessions; his aversion to certain fabrics, the comfort he found in a weighty blanket, and an extraordinarily picky palate. Tyler wouldn't eat what we put in front of him until he fell into that state between wakefulness and sleep—head down on his high-chair table, eyes shut, as he slowly shoveled food into his mouth. The rest of the family would tiptoe around the high chair while clearing the dinner table, knowing that if Tyler woke up, he'd stop eating.

It was all so adorable. After his diagnosis, I learned that the pediatrician who first identified Tyler's form of autism, Hans Asperger, called kids like Tyler "little professors," because of their unusually sophisticated vocabularies. Dr. Tony Attwood, author of *The Complete Guide to Asperger's Syndrome*, said Aspies lack "social understanding" and harbor intense interest in one or two subjects. "Perhaps the simplest way to understand Asperger's syndrome is to think of it as describing someone who perceives and thinks about the world differently to other people."

They're wired differently. With the right support, Aspies can lead loving and productive lives. They need to learn how to read body language, how to modulate their voices, and how to follow the subtle rules of conversation and relationships.

Tyler tried. Once he noticed Lori's eyes welling after she received some good news. "Those are happy tears, right?" he asked. "You know, sometimes I can't tell the difference."

In his charming and brutally honest memoir about his late-in-life Asperger's diagnosis, *The Journal of Best Practices*, David Finch wrote, "Most people intuitively know how to function and interact with people—they don't need to learn it by rote. I do." He described his natural conversational style as verbose, exhausting, and unfiltered—"the verbal equivalent of a volcanic eruption, spewing mind magma in every direction."

Bestselling author Temple Grandin warned that Aspies like herself "are often loners, with few friends, the geeks, the nerds, the socially odd individuals who never seem to fit in." She urged parents and educators to aggressively identify children with Asperger's. In *The Way I See It,* Grandin explained: "The worst thing parents can do with a child between the ages of 2–5 is nothing." Reading that sentence makes me sick to my stomach. Tyler was 12 before we did something.

Why did it take so long? The most benign explanation is that Asperger's is easy to overlook because Aspies are so well-spoken and intelligent, according to Grandin and other experts, especially when it comes to their favorite subjects.

Another excuse: We were enchanted. You've heard the expression "Kids say the darnedest things." They all do. But kids with Tyler's particular wiring are uniquely bright and expressive, which makes them hypnotizing. His sister Gabrielle once caught me at the dinner table staring at Tyler and joked, "You look at him like he's the Christ-child." He wasn't the son of God, of course, but I knew from the get-go that this son of mine was special. He amazed me. He also worried me. Which touches on a darker explanation for our neglect, or mine, anyway: I didn't want to believe that Tyler was clinically, certifiably *different*.

BRICK HECK IS a geek: a scrawny and bookish youngest child who whispers observations to himself, partly because he has no friends who might listen. A young character in the ABC sitcom *The Middle*, Brick reminds me more of Tyler than does Max Braverman, because Brick's apparent autism is milder than Max's. Adults love Brick. Kids steer clear of him. His parents struggle to understand and help him. In one of the show's earliest episodes, Brick's dad realizes that he is just as "socially challenged" as his son. The pair screw up the nerve to attend a block party, then later commiserate about their relative success.

"Maybe we're meant to be who we're meant to be, and it's when we start trying to change who we're meant to be that things get messed up," the father says. "Brick, are you happy?"

"Yes," Brick replies. "Are you happy?"

"Yes. So why are we letting people try to change us?" In other words, different is okay.

Try telling that to Adam Bromberg, Stacey's husband. "My wife, she's taken it hard." We were eating lunch at an Alexandria, Virginia, restaurant, a few weeks before I met his wife at Starbucks. "Her problem isn't the diagnosis as much as the fact that Gavin doesn't fit in socially and so on. She takes it more personally." But he takes it personally, too. "My job was to raise him, and I should have seen something sooner. I should have done more."

Why didn't he? "I don't know," Adam replied. "We saw things, little things, but we just didn't want to believe that something could be wrong with our little boy." It's a common refrain in my conversation with parents.

Through Twitter, I met Craig S., a North Carolina businessman raising teenage triplets, one of whom has a bundle of issues that sound to him like mild autism. He has hesitated to seek a diagnosis, much less treatment, because he can't let his dreams go. "I grew up a jock. My dad and I connected through sports and it was a bond for us. My kid has zero interest [in sports]. Not just a little—zero."

"He's not like you," I said, "and if you're right, your boy is autistic and needs help."

"I hate to even think about that," he replied.

A few weeks later, I met John S. in a grungy Mexican restaurant not far from the attorney general's office in Lansing, Michigan, where John works as a spokesman. He is a divorced father with a mildly autistic son. We were eating tacos and drinking beer. "There's these puzzle pieces scattered . . ." John stopped for five seconds, his face reddening. "I said I wasn't going to cry about this." We took a pull on our beers.

"I'm sorry. I do it all the time," he said, blotting his eyes with a napkin. "It came fast."

While he regained his composure, I told John that the puzzle piece is a symbol for autism. "It's fitting," he said. "Because to me there are things scattered all over the table. You know, when he was born everything looked good, but he didn't want to be held. His mom finally gave him a swaddling blanket, because he would kick and scream whenever we put him to bed. But he hated the blanket. He can't stand being trapped in any way. That was a puzzle piece I didn't know what to do with."

John continued: "The little professor stuff—I remember he was probably as little as 3, walking down the street in Charlevoix [Michigan] on vacation, just charming the daylights out of adults. So you'd be like, 'I've got the greatest kid and things are going to be awesome.'"

But they weren't awesome. They weren't perfect. Not for John or for me—or for any parent, really. You can hear our kids in the lyrics of singer-songwriter Roger Miller: *Funny I don't fit. Where have all the average people gone?* The only thing normal about any child is that *something* makes him or her different.

Malia and Sasha have a perspective that is typical of
their generation: They take for granted that treating
somebody differently because of their race makes
no sense, in the same way they take for granted
that it doesn't make sense to treat somebody
differently because of their sexual orientation or
disability. It doesn't require a lecture for them.

BARACK OBAMA, TO *PEOPLE* MAGAZINE,
DECEMBER 2014

2

GENIUS

"If He Falls Behind Now, He Won't Get into the Right Middle School"

Quincy, Massachusetts—*Now that we had checked off Lori's first box with the White House trip, it was my turn— and I knew where I would take Tyler next: the homestead of John Adams and his son John Quincy Adams. The nation's second and sixth presidents, respectively, the Adamses were the only father and son to hold that office until George H. W. Bush and George W. Bush started calling each other "41" and "43."*

Years ago, I was researching the history of education in America when I came across a revealing story about the relationship between John and John Q. When the younger Adams was 7 years old, his father wrote home from Philadelphia, where the elder Adams and other delegates from the 13 American colonies were debating whether to declare independence from Britain. The father had another matter on his mind: his aspirations for the education of his four children. "Let us teach them not only to do virtuously, but to excel," he wrote his wife, Abigail. "To excel, they must be taught to be steady, active, and industrious." Soon after, John Q. wrote to his father that he was working hard at his studies and hoped "to grow into a better boy."

I find something uncomfortably familiar in the elder Adams' exacting expectations and his son's desperate vow. John Q. might as well have written, "I hope I don't let you down, Dad." I try to talk to Tyler about it today while touring Quincy, but he won't. He doesn't like to talk about his feelings and has developed numerous defensive mechanisms to keep people at bay. One is humor. Another is the filibuster: When Tyler gets nervous, he fixes on a subject and talks it to death. Today it's the elder Adams. "I learned somewhere that he lived to be 90," Tyler says, pointing to a picture of the elder Adams hanging in a hotel lobby, where we're having lunch before touring the Adams property. "Keep in mind, that was a time when people usually lived to be 45 before kicking the bucket. He died on July 4, Dad. The same exact day as Thomas Jefferson. They hated each other until they got old, and wrote a great series of letters." The words are pouring out of Tyler's mind now, faster than his lips can move, collapsing upon each other in a barely understandable torrent. "You know what John Adams' final words were?"

I shake my head.

"Thomas Jefferson survives." Tyler laughs. "What a diss!"

He had tried to back out of the tour earlier in the day, preferring to spend the day alone in the hotel room, but he's now engaged in conversation—progress, already. Actually, it's more of a monologue. As if his brain is a website being queried for presidential information, Tyler pulls up fact after somewhat-related fact. The elder Adams was a lawyer who defended British officers accused of the Boston Massacre murders. He wrote the Massachusetts constitution, a model for the U.S. document. The Tea Party was just a tax fight. And on and on . . .

"The Tea Party is a weird name. When you think of 'tea party,' you think of a refined class. But it was just a bunch of thugs throwing tea into the harbor and . . ." Tyler stops and stares at me. "You're not listening." He's right, I'm not.

"Yes I am."

"What did I just say?"

I shrug. "Something about the Tea Party?" Tyler laughs again. He's accustomed to people tuning him out, in part because, as a person with Asperger's, Tyler has a difficult time understanding whether people are interested in what he has to say. "Let's go on the tour," I say.

The Adams National Historic Park consists of three homes. The saltbox house where John Adams was born is located just 75 feet from the birthplace of his son, and both sit hard against what is now a busy suburban street—so close to the road that from inside the 18th-century homes you can hear music booming from the fast-passing cars. The third structure is called the Old House, a sprawling two-story home to both

John Adams and John Quincy Adams. We start at the tiny saltbox house, where Tyler keeps interrupting to correct the park ranger, ask a question, or crack a joke.

"Is this actually the real house?" Tyler's right hand is in the air. He's the only child in a clutch of 13 tourists.

"Good question." The ranger raises an eyebrow, impressed. "I don't get that one asked often."

Tyler pushes. "If I had been here when Adams was 13, I would have seen these same things?"

"Actually, the main skeleton—the beams and foundation—is original," the ranger replies, "but much of the rest is an authentic reproduction."

Tyler grimaces. "Authentic? Reproduction? Those words don't match."

"Guilty," the ranger chuckles.

I cringe. "Give somebody else a chance to speak, son." I'm worried that he's dominating the tour and irritating the adults.

"Okay, Dad."

We file onto a bus and drive to the Old House, also called Peacefield, where I slip my arm around Tyler's shoulders, something he hasn't allowed me to do since he was a toddler. He lets it linger while we walk from a large second-floor study to a long hallway and parlor on the ground floor, and then outside to the Stone Library.

The Gothic Revival library has two rings of books: One wraps around a magnificent black-and-white checkerboard floor, and the other towers above and is rimmed by a gated wood walkway. The library holds personal papers and

12,000 books that belonged to John Adams, John Quincy Adams, and other family members. Not among the papers, but housed at the nearby Massachusetts Historical Society, is the April 23, 1794, letter John Adams once wrote to his young son, who had expressed a wish to lead the simple life of an attorney. "You come into life with advantages which disgrace you, if your success is mediocre," the elder Adams wrote.

Outside the library, everybody introduces themselves. A white-haired lady, a retired teacher who stands five feet tall in heels, says to nobody in particular, "What happened to that nice young fellow with all the smart questions?" I don't know whom she's talking about. "Oh, there he is!" She points to Tyler. "When I didn't hear you ask any more questions, I assumed you had left." Her eyes narrow at me. "You didn't tell him to shush, did you?"

I nod, and feel blood rushing to my face.

She said, "Why did you shush your boy?"

I shrug as she slowly turns to Tyler. Her shoulders are coiled, and it looks like it hurts her to stand; she winces in the pivot from me to Tyler. "I love your curious mind," she says to him. "What's your name?"

"Tyler." He looks into the lady's eyes and shakes her hand—two unnatural acts for somebody with Asperger's. More progress.

Since his diagnosis less than a year ago, Tyler has begun taking social skills classes to learn, among other things, how to introduce himself, and also to understand how he's perceived by other people. I'm learning, too—specifically, to see Tyler

through the eyes of others. That nice young fellow with all the
smart questions? That's my boy. He's funny and charming
and sweet and blessed with extraordinary intellect that he'll
learn to harness—even if he does so in ways that defy my
dreams for him. I need to learn to deal with those expectations.
I don't want Tyler to be like the younger Adams—stalked for
life by the charge to "grow into a better boy."

I LOVE THE first day of school. It's a time of possibility
and hope—a milestone, not unlike a child's birthday,
that gives parents an opportunity to mark progress. I
never missed a first day of school. A particularly memorable one was September 2, 2003, when Gabrielle entered middle school and Tyler began kindergarten.

Gabrielle wore her hair in a braid and walked into
her new school shoulder to shoulder with Holly, who
wanted to show her sister around before starting her
second year of high school. Then Lori and I took Tyler
to kindergarten.

"See ya, Dad!" he said, walking into his classroom.

Lori showed Tyler where to hang his backpack and
store his SpongeBob SquarePants lunchbox. "Love
you, son."

"Love you, too, Mom."

Lori and I shuffled our feet and smiled. We didn't
want to leave. Surely he needed more help, or hugs and

kisses. In a flat baritone that belied his age, Tyler told us, "You can go now."

That evening I rushed home from work in time for dinner, and Gabrielle greeted me at the door. "I had a great day!" she squealed, throwing her arms around my neck. The five of us gathered to eat while Gabrielle gossiped about the girl in school with green hair ("Stay away from her," Lori said) and another with a nose ring ("Stay away from her, too!").

Tyler said he had a "great day" and told us about a blond girl in his class. "She's cute," he said. "I'm going to marry her." He said he'd sat next to a boy with the same SpongeBob lunchbox. "He's going to be my best friend." Listening to her younger siblings, Holly smiled and nodded. She was a straight-A student, a good athlete, and a pretty, blue-eyed blonde. From all appearances, she was the ideal, trouble-free teen—so strong and confident, immune to typical teenage pressures. "I had a great day, too."

Lori and I caught each other's eye and smiled. Everything was perfect.

OF ALL GOOGLE searches starting "Is my 2-year-old . . . ," the most common next word is "gifted," according to Seth Stephens-Davidowitz, a writer and economist who studied aggregate data from Google searches. "It's hardly surprising," he wrote in the *New*

York Times, "that parents of young children are often excited at the thought that their child may be gifted."

Excited, sure. But, mostly, anxious. "They gave my 4-year-old an IQ test the other day," said Laura M., a friend of mine whose son had just been diagnosed with dyspraxia, a developmental coordination disorder that makes it difficult for him to stay on task at school. Laura had invited me to lunch to get my advice. "He scored 95," she said, dragging her salad around her plate.

I said, "That's probably about where I scored on my IQ."

"But that's *average*." Laura spat out the last word like a curse.

Intellect is no longer a gift to parents like Laura. It's a commodity. If moms and dads had their way, genius would be a standard accessory; every kid would be one. We look at the global competition for jobs and pray that our kid gets an intellectual leg up. We're influenced by pop culture's celebration of prodigies, and we think, *My little one is just as smart.* And as much as we hate to admit it, most of us moms and dads still are tangled in our educational histories. If you're an Ivy League graduate, you probably expect the same gilded path for your child. Universities play to that conceit by offering the children of its graduates "legacy admission" advantages. For the rest of us—parents like Lori and me, who graduated from second-tier colleges, or those parents who didn't go to college at all—there's a temptation to push our kids farther than we could go.

Part of the appeal of raising brainy sophisticates comes from Hollywood, where smart is the new sexy. Shows such as *The Big Bang Theory, Community, Futurama*, and *The IT Crowd* mock ignorance and celebrate genius. *The Big Bang Theory* revolves around Sheldon Cooper, a physicist whose arrogant genius is a running punch line. In one episode, Sheldon's roommate, the marginally less geeky Leonard, wears an Apple store T-shirt for hot nerd cred. A friend says, "You were pretending to work at the Genius Bar to pick up women, weren't you?"

Schools are where we house our hefty intellectual expectations. From preschool to graduate school, the American education system is an assembly line of angst—pressure on parents to prepare their kids for global combat, pressure on kids to achieve, and pressure on educators squeezed between competing demands: *Drive our kids to excel,* parents tell them, *but don't drive them too hard or, heaven forbid, allow them to fail.* The result is a generation of kids who are both pushed and protected.

Push: The class of 2013 took 3.2 million Advanced Placement exams, according to a College Board survey of U.S. public schools, nearly double the 2003 total. Parents seek a tuition-free head start on college for their kids.

Protect: Parents lobby teachers to reduce home-work workloads, even for AP students.

Push: Parents demand higher education standards.

Protect: Parents punish educators for their kids' poor grades, and schools react by artificially inflating grades and promoting kids who should be held back.

Push: Parents pay for expensive SAT prep courses, hire college-admission counselors, and strategically contribute to college endowments.

Protect: Helicopter parents hover at college, decorating dorms, wiring cash, and nagging professors.

NOT THAT LONG ago, school was a luxury. Now it's a necessity, which creates certain pressures. In the early 19th century, less than half of all 5-to-19-year-olds enrolled in school, rising to 51 percent in 1900 and to 75 percent in 1940 as child labor laws chased young minds out of the workplace. By 2014, some 21 million students attended U.S. colleges and universities, an increase of about 5.7 million since 2000, according to the National Center for Education Statistics. Meanwhile, the dropout rate among 16-through-24-year-olds had declined from 10.9 percent in 2000 to 6.6 percent a dozen years later.

My niece Anna was in *seventh grade* when she took her first ACT test for college, scoring a point higher than I did 30 years ago as a *high school senior*. Through the Duke University Talent Identification Program (TIP), Anna won a gold medal and a small scholarship to the University of Arkansas at Little Rock, in her hometown. She and a couple dozen other young Einsteins were honored at a campus ceremony where the keynote speaker, Megan Chung, a 16-year-old alum of the TIP program, revealed how her "tiger mom" had pushed her to excel in school and at the piano.

"Parents," Megan giggled. "I'm not saying you should force activities and grades on your children. Students, I *am* saying you should force your parents to let you do this program." She told the seventh-graders to aim high. "It is never too early to start thinking about college. Remember, time is ticking away."

Parents don't need a reminder. They hear the clock ticking. I know a single father in Alabama who adopted a boy from Guatemala, now a seventh-grade student pulling down straight A's. The dad joined the PTA, lavished the boy's teachers with gifts, and equipped his son with thousands of dollars in education-related technology. Four years before he would take an actual college entrance exam, the boy sat for an SAT prep test.

"You're going to get a college scholarship," the father told the boy at dinner. "You've got to get a college scholarship."

The boy excused himself from the table. "I've got a stomachache again."

In our neighborhood, parents pay tutors $50 an hour to keep their kids in Advanced Placement classes. "If you have to pay a tutor to load up Andy's plate," Lori gently suggested to a fellow mom, "maybe he doesn't belong in an AP class."

At one elite high school in nearby Fairfax, Virginia, according to the *Washington Post*, a Korean math prodigy forged communications from Harvard and Princeton to convince her parents, teachers, and eventually the world media that she had earned duel admission to both Ivies. "We celebrate the accomplishments of students who get into all eight Ivies," said Brandon Kosatka, director of student services at Thomas Jefferson High School for Science and Technology, where the young woman dubbed "Genius Girl" concocted her hoax. "If that's the bar, then, yes, that creates anxiety for them."

In Silicon Valley, the students are so hyped-up and stressed-out over grades that one high school has created a sleep curriculum, hiring sleep experts and training students as "sleep ambassadors." Drowsy school children are a national epidemic: 55 percent of American teenagers from the ages 14 to 17 reported they were getting fewer than seven hours of sleep a night, according to a study in the *Medical Journal of Pediatrics*. "I've got kids on a regular basis telling me that they're getting five hours," Denise Pope, co-author

of *Overloaded and Underprepared,* told columnist Frank
Bruni of the *New York Times.* That endangers their
mental and physical health.

John S., the Michigan dad I met in Lansing for
tacos and beer, told me that his son recently had been
expelled from a suburban elementary school for disruptive behavior. John suspected it was a ruse. His son
has learning disabilities, and John believed that school
administrators acted to eliminate a threat to their academic ratings. "This was real emotional for me, because I was a huge failure," John said. "How . . ." He
paused. "How is it that I send my kid to what I thought
was the best school and they're rejecting him?" His
voice trembled to a whisper. "Dammit."

What John said next was a testament to our era
of not-so-great expectations. "If he falls behind now,
he won't get in the right middle school, which means
he won't get in the right high school, which means he
won't get in the right college," he said. "He needs to
be succeeding—*now.*"

THE RAW INTENSITY of parental aspirations reverber-
ates beyond the classrooms. Bowing to demands for
better schools, Democratic and Republican political leaders in the 1980s embraced the idea of national
standards and accountability in public education. Decades later, the nation's governors and corporate leaders joined forces to develop what came to be known

as Common Core State Standards, a package of goals, curriculum, and testing that would be internationally competitive.

The Common Core was popular at first, adopted by 45 states and the District of Columbia, but parents hadn't read the fine print. For one thing, when schools shift to standardized tests based on a common curriculum, scores generally fall. Education Secretary Arne Duncan had warned that this would happen—lower scores are a price parents must pay for tougher, better schools.

Predictably, the first whiff of declining scores stirred howls of protest, and the once popular reforms faced an uncertain future. Duncan lashed out. "It's fascinating to me that some of the pushback is coming from, sort of, white suburban moms who—all of a sudden—their child isn't as brilliant as they thought they were and their school isn't quite as good as they thought they were, and that's pretty scary," Duncan said. "You've bet your house and where you live and everything on, 'My child's going to be prepared.' That can be a punch in the gut."

The terror of expectations—"My child's going to be prepared!"—exposes parents to exploitation. Entire industries prey upon mothers and fathers desperately dodging what Duncan called a "gut punch"—the sudden realization that a child isn't perfect, or perfectly prepared for the world.

For instance, the market for education software

exploded in 2012, with nearly 50,000 developers cranking out computer apps that sing nursery rhymes to children, coach them to say words, and teach them foreign languages. Consumer groups have accused the multibillion-dollar industry of feasting on the fears and hopes of parents by peddling technology that often doesn't work.

Elite day care centers and preschools boast of waiting lists that are months if not years long. Jockeying for admission often begins before pregnancy. Intensive student tests, family background checks, and high tuition fees all give certain day cares a patina of elitism that tempts lower- and middle-class parents to bolt from their no-frills day cares. Doing so will assuredly bust their budgets, with no guarantee of significantly better services.

The college-admission process is a "great, brutal culling," according to author Frank Bruni, who exposes a consort of deceit perpetrated by colleges and college-ranking systems. In *Where You Go Is Not Who You'll Be: An Antidote to the College Admission Mania*, the *New York Times* columnist argues that the nature of a student's college experience—"the work that he or she puts into it, the skills that he or she picks up, the self-examination that's undertaken, the resourcefulness that's honed"—matters more than the reputation of the institution he or she attends.

Even the journalism business—my profession—

exploits prodding parents through stories that author Amanda Hess calls "parental hate-reads," clickbait aimed at competitive mothers and fathers: stories about parents who hire $2,500 nanny consulting services, who enlist artist-babysitters at $5 to $15 more an hour than the average sitter, who shift from high school PTA leadership posts to volunteering at the admissions office at the college their kid attends. "We hold up a new set of moms and dads for a round of public shaming (or, in the case of the first-person diatribe, self-flagellation)," Hess wrote for *Slate*.

Finally, the makers and sellers of attention-deficit medication may be benefiting from the academic expectations boom. The National Health Interview Survey reported in 2010 that 8.4 percent of children, or 5.2 million, had been diagnosed with attention-deficit/hyperactivity disorder. Those are huge numbers compared to 1980, when just 3 percent of children were thought to suffer from ADHD. Ritalin production soared 500 percent between 1990 and 1996, according to Peter N. Stearns' *Anxious Parents*, which also catalogued the rise in academic expectations.

While it's a stretch to say parents are doping their kids solely to achieve academic success, a combination of scientific advances and social pressures have created a convenient cocktail for indirect and unintended abuses. In a *New York Times* essay titled "Raising the Ritalin Generation," author Bronwen Hruska quoted

one of her son's teachers suggesting, "Just a little medication could really turn things around for Will." The
final paragraphs of her August 2012 essay drew a direct
link between academic expectations and drugs.

> If "accelerated" has become the new normal,
> there's no choice but to diagnose the kids devel-
> oping at a normal rate with a disorder. Instead
> of leveling the playing field for kids who really
> do suffer from a deficit, we're ratcheting up the
> level of competition with performance-enhancing
> drugs. We're juicing our kids for school.
>
> We're also ensuring that down the road, when
> faced with other challenges that high school, col-
> lege, and adult life are sure to bring, our chil-
> dren will use the coping skills we've taught them.
> They'll reach for a pill.

EVER HEAR THE metaphor of a boiling frog? If a frog
is placed in boiling water, it will jump out and escape,
but if it is placed in cold water that slowly is heated, it
won't notice the danger and will be cooked to death.
The anecdote is used to describe the inability or un-
willingness of people to react to drastic changes that
occur gradually. Holly was a boiling frog.

When she started middle school, our eldest daughter suffered nervous episodes over her grades and
homework, sometimes to the point of vomiting. We

chalked that up to teenage angst. Lori thought Holly would learn to manage her nerves; I thought she would toughen up. Lori did what she could for Holly; I did what I could from the campaign trail, where I spent large chunks of Holly's middle school years. We had no doubt things would work out. After all, Holly was a great kid.

At Yorktown High, a public school located in the affluent suburbs just outside Washington, our oldest daughter drifted away from elementary school friends and began spending most of her time with a new friend, a girl from a single-parent home who struggled, like Holly, with expectations at home and at school.

Holly was driven to excel. Lori tells a funny story about the day Holly brought home a pile of vole bones encased in owl vomit, with instructions from her science teacher to assemble the rodent remains into a standing skeleton. Lori and Holly quickly assembled the bones—foot to ankle to thigh to hip to chest to skull. Try as they might, though, mother and daughter couldn't get the skeleton to stand.

After several hours, Lori sighed, "We did the best we could. Your teacher will just have to accept it lying down."

Holly said, "No. She said she'll mark us down a full grade if it doesn't stand up. I don't want a B."

"Nothing wrong with a B," Lori chuckled. "Your dad got plenty of them, and he did all right."

Holly sobbed, "I can't get a B." She was inconsolable,

but the vole and Lori were just as stubborn. Holly got a B.

While Holly was obsessed with getting great grades and being admitted to a top college, Lori and I didn't care much about where she went to school. We did fine with our commuter-college degrees. So if not us, what drove Holly?

I suspect part of the problem was her genes. Her father is insanely competitive and comes from a family of win-at-all-cost warriors. Holly could have benefited from more of her mother's genetic influence. Another culprit was the culture of the Arlington County School District, an affluent and nationally recognized public school system, where parents, teachers, and peers demanded excellence.

Years later, Holly said, "It wasn't so much what my teachers wanted from me, because what they wanted was high test scores and good grades, and I got those anyway. It was what they weren't giving me: any sort of warmth or any sort of caring about me as a person." Holly had missed a lot of high school because of her nerves, and her nerves were on edge because of problems at home. Holly was fighting with Gabrielle, with whom she shared a room, and we responded to the fights by yelling at both girls. Gabrielle shrugged off conflict. Holly internalized it, and slowly convinced herself that she wasn't loved or liked.

I should have seen this coming. A friend of mine,

Scott Gilbride, had a daughter who was drowning in her own expectations. Mary Lacey Gilbride was a star athlete and straight-A student who played pickup basketball on Monday nights with several men, including me and her father. One night, while we watched Mary Lacey warm up with a blizzard of three-point shots, Scott asked about Holly. Our girls were about the same age, and we liked to compare notes. "She's fine," I said. "But, boy, she's getting moody. She's fighting with her sister and mom all the time."

"Daughters are glorious," said Scott, the father of three girls, "but they're never easy." A few weeks later, after three long and sloppy pickup games, Scott confided in me, "Mary Lacey has talked about killing herself. We don't know what to do." He fretted about the drugs prescribed to her—none of them had worked for long. He complained that mental health research was underappreciated and underfunded. "We need more research into mental illness," Scott said, "and parents need to be taught how not to miss the signs of severe depression."

I had missed them. Lori and I thought we just had a snotty teenager on our hands. We didn't know Holly was depressed. Neither did school officials. "None of those teachers asked me if I was okay when I missed all that school," Holly said of her middle school issues. In high school, "teachers spent their time helping the struggling kids or the bad kids. Meanwhile, I'm getting good grades and being quiet and nobody paid attention to me until . . ." Holly paused. "It was almost too late."

It was almost too late. Just writing that sentence gives me a chill. In mid-January of Holly's senior year, I was working out of the house on a school day when the phone rang. I answered it. "Mr. Fournier?" It was Holly's counselor. "Your daughter's in my office, sir. She's been talking about hurting herself."

"What do you mean, hurting herself?" I had no clue.

"She's told a teacher and a friend that she's thinking of killing herself."

Urgently, we got Holly help. Her mental health stabilized enough that, just seven months after her breakdown, we drove two hours from our home and dropped her off at James Madison University. And prayed.

IN ELEMENTARY SCHOOL, Tyler asked Lori what she thought of his second-grade teacher. "She is nice," Lori replied. Tyler's eyes, two sea-blue globes, widened in alarm. "Mom, you don't know her!" he protested. "She has a dark side." We laughed, which might seem odd, but we knew he was being hyperbolic. The teacher wasn't evil; she simply was frustrated with Tyler's academic progress, and for good reason. Despite his obvious intellectual precociousness, Tyler was sinking in school.

His IQ is higher than that of 98 percent of the population, nearly genius-level. His recall of facts is nearly perfect, especially with regard to his favorite topics. He entered elementary school with an adult-level vocabulary. All this increased our expectations for Tyler, his teachers, and ourselves. Why isn't this little genius getting better grades?

He rarely completed assignments, and often didn't start them. During the teacher's lectures, Tyler stared out the window—when he wasn't interrupting. Reading came hard to him until he discovered video game strategy guides, and for the longest time, that's all he would read. Most alarming to Lori and me was his inability to put thoughts on paper. The kid couldn't write. Part of the problem seemed to be fine motor skills. He simply couldn't manage the act of holding a pencil and directing his hand to create letters, words, and sentences on paper. But even when we asked him to dictate to us, Tyler froze. He could talk in full, rich paragraphs every waking minute until we said, "Okay, it's time for homework."

The teacher blamed it on his attention issues and recommended to Lori that we hire a nutritionist. The nutritionist put Tyler on a diet of organic foods, none of which we could get him to eat. From the time he graduated from baby foods, Tyler's diet had consisted of just five items: Velveeta macaroni and cheese (the kind with shell noodles—no other shape would do), hot dogs (only Oscar Mayer "classic"), fish sticks, bananas, and chocolate Pop-Tarts. That was it. Nothing we did could convince Tyler to try something new, particularly organic hot dogs and gluten-free macaroni and cheese.

His aversion to new food mystified us, but we shrugged it off. Some kids are picky eaters. *He'll grow out of it.* We didn't recognize that his sensitive palate was a red flag. Instead, we focused on a question that had long divided us: Do we put him on attention-deficit medication? Lori and I fought over this more than almost anything else in our marriage. She wanted him medicated. I didn't.

"If he had diabetes or high blood pressure, you wouldn't think twice about giving him drugs," she told me. Lori was singularly equipped to understand the depths of Tyler's problems because, with rare exceptions, she was the only parent who struggled with him over homework, met with teachers, and took him to doctor's appointments.

She saw Tyler as a revving engine that couldn't slow down. Lori cried whenever she thought what life must like for Tyler amid such inner turmoil. "You have no idea what he's going through," Lori told me. "You have no idea how badly he needs help."

My opposition to attention-deficit medicine was purely visceral, informed by parental hate-reads and blind machismo. I declared, "We're not drugging my son."

We drugged my son. He was finishing second grade when I finally conceded that Tyler couldn't learn if he couldn't focus, and he couldn't focus without medication. Lori worked aggressively with the doctor, constantly tweaking medication types and levels. Too little and the medication didn't help. Too much and the drugs made Tyler flat, like a zombie. His prescription changed every few months as his chemistry adjusted with age. Lori's advocacy stopped Tyler's academic slide, but he struggled in school for many more years, especially with the writing, until Dr. Quinn's diagnosis—and our guilt trips—put him on a better path.

ACADEMIC EXPECTATIONS COMPLICATED an already challenging environment for Tyler. Parents pressured political leaders to raise test scores and college admission percentages. Politicians pressured school administrators. School administrators pressured teachers. Teachers pampered the brightest students and buoyed the failing ones, which left little bandwidth for kids like Tyler in the mushy middle. His disruptive behavior, as much a part of Tyler as his autism, didn't win any friends in the teachers' lounge.

Academic expectations robbed Holly of the emotional support she needed in high school. Her teachers and parents were focused on her grades, not her mental well-being. We dodged a bullet. Holly graduated from college, started a career, and got married. She now works for the *Detroit News*, thriving professionally and personally.

Lori and I were blessed with the means to hire tutors and therapists to fix what the schools broke or couldn't fix. For other parents, the stakes and costs are much steeper.

In our lust for academic excellence, we forget the pride and promise of our children's first day of school. It is not their destiny on that September day to be the smartest or most accomplished children. It is their time to learn. To learn to be their best, not their best impression of what we want them to be. The next parent who Googles "Is my 2-year-old gifted?" should get a curt response: "Your 2-year-old is a gift."

> If you do not rise to the head not only of your profession, but of your country, it will be owing to your own laziness, slovenliness and obstinacy.
>
> JOHN ADAMS, IN A LETTER TO HIS SON
> JOHN QUINCY ADAMS, APRIL 23, 1794

3

POPULAR

"I Thought I Could Buy Them Friends"

Cove Neck, New York—*This isn't right. It is 55 degrees and sunny, a perfect late autumn morning in suburban New York, and I'm on the road with my boy. But something's off. The electronic navigator that guided us 250 miles to the former hometown of Theodore Roosevelt is now telling us in a soothing robotic voice to stop here, in front of a 1,000-square-foot ranch house with slate-gray siding and butter-yellow shutters. "You . . . have . . . arrived." Stationed at the edge of a burnt lawn is one of those bent-over wooden garden women. I tell Tyler, "I don't think this is TR's house."*

"No joke," Tyler laughs. "I'm bored. Just kidding." On the ride here, Tyler had complained repeatedly about being pulled away from his video games and books, until I finally told him to knock it off. Now he's got me laughing at myself. I reprogram the navigator for 20 Sagamore Hill and we drive another 10 minutes.

Sagamore Hill National Park is 83 acres of forestland, meadows, and salt marshes overlooking Oyster Bay Harbor and Long Island Sound. In addition to nature trails, a boardwalk, an icehouse, and a pet cemetery, the property includes two homes. The grandest was completed in 1886 under Theodore Roosevelt's direction and expanded in 1905 to add the largest of its 23 rooms, the North Room. Tyler is fascinated by the menagerie of animal detritus, including elephant tusks, a stuffed badger, and a polar bear rug, all nods to Roosevelt's passion for hunting. Tyler observes with a laugh, "This is a zoo for the dead."

We're here because Roosevelt is Tyler's favorite president, though I'm not sure why that is. On the drive, I had asked Tyler whether he identified with Roosevelt because TR was a sickly child. Tyler stared out the windshield at the approaching Manhattan skyline. "No," he mumbled.

Well, was it because, as a boy, TR was taunted by classmates?

"No."

Was it because both of them loved animals and science and history?

"Nope." *Tyler cut me off.* "He was just cool, man. Kids don't have to have reasons. He was just a cool dude."

We start our tour at the smallest building, closest to the parking lot. The park's museum is in the Orchard House, a Georgian-style mansion built in 1937–38 by Ted Roosevelt Jr. A musty smell and a well-worn gray carpet greet us at the door, yielding to high-ceilinged rooms stuffed with exhibits. Next to the first interior door is a clear plastic

case, empty but for a crinkled five-dollar bill. A sign reads
DONATIONS.

The first exhibit commemorates February 14, 1884, the day Roosevelt's beloved mother, Martha Bulloch Roosevelt, and his first wife, Alice Hathaway Lee Roosevelt, died within hours of each other. Roosevelt wrote in his diary that night, "The light has gone out in my life." He hardly spoke of Alice again.

A knot of tourists at the exhibit share funereal whispers until startled by Tyler's booming voice. "Talk about a hard day!" he laughs. "Two for the price of one!" This is what they call a learning moment, exactly what Lori had in mind when she conceived of the road trips. Help him read people, she said, and understand when jokes are appropriate and when they're not. Yeah, well, that's going to have to wait until we get back to the hotel.

I nudge him, say, "Be respectful, son," and nod apologetically to the tourists.

We move quickly to the exhibit on Roosevelt's childhood— his debilitating asthma, his scrawny build, and a reference to two boys who bullied him on a camping trip. I think of Tyler—his Asperger's, his social awkwardness, and the bullying he is starting to experience. It's not physical, at least as far as we know, but middle school is the age at which kids are most likely to be the source and subject of verbal abuse. At 13, even as an Aspie, Tyler is now self-aware enough to understand that he's a target.

I delicately ask, "What do you think?"

He chuckles. "I think you're trying too hard."

We leave the childhood exhibit for one about Roosevelt's time in the American West—buckskins, branding irons, buffalo guns, and other tokens of wide-open spaces sealed inside a glass box. There's a box for every chapter of Roosevelt's expansive life: fighting political patronage via the U.S. Civil Service Commission, exposing corruption as New York's police chief, preparing the nation for war at the Navy Department, leading the Rough Riders in the Spanish-American War, and returning home a hero to defy the New York political machine and become a reformist governor. Wanting him out of Albany, GOP bosses made Roosevelt the party's vice presidential nominee in 1900. The move backfired when an anarchist assassinated President William McKinley in September 1901, making Roosevelt the nation's youngest-ever president at age 42.

The foreign policy exhibit, titled "Stepping onto the World Stage," triggers a thought. Roosevelt led the United States away from its isolationist instincts and into the global community, stronger and more confident than at any previous time in its history. Tyler is just starting to learn how to emerge from his shell and embrace the broader community. I excitedly share my theory: "America had Asperger's and TR showed the country how to cope."

Tyler chuckles again. "Nice try."

Desperate now, I point to a picture of an adoring crowd of thousands cheering the toothy Roosevelt. "He was sick and mostly alone as a kid but then grew up to be wildly popular. Do you want to be popular, buddy? Do you want more friends?"

*"That is not why he's my favorite president. He's my
favorite president because he kicked butt!"*

*"Do you want to kick butt, buddy? Roosevelt muscled up
so he could fight bullies. Do you want to muscle up?"*

"No," he says with a shrug.

"But—"

"Dad, stop." His tone is flat, firm. For a moment it feels
like we have reversed roles and my son is now teaching me.
He says, *"Remember the* Freaks *book?"* Just 10 days ago,
Tyler brought home from school a memoir, Freaks, Geeks
and Asperger Syndrome, and pointed to a passage. *"First
of all,"* the 13-year-old author, Luke Jackson, wrote, *"the
biggest gem of advice I can give you on this subject is never
force your child to socialize."* The boy author added, *"Most
AS and autistic people are happy just to be by themselves and
do their own thing, rather than going out and meeting people
and having people around for social occasions. On the con-
trary, this makes them nervous—at least it does me and other
AS people I know."*

"Remember the book?" Tyler repeats.

I nod as I stare at the picture of Roosevelt. *"I remember,
buddy."*

*"I'm happy by myself, Dad. You don't have to force
things so much."*

TYLER AND I were park rats. Our neighborhood in
northern Virginia was flush with playgrounds, and

we loved to explore them after work and on my days off. Tyler had nicknames for each one: "House Park," "Super Park," "Yellow Park," and so on. I would crawl with Tyler up and around the hard plastic equipment, or we would play imagination games together. But more often than not, Tyler would play without me, which is why I always brought a book. From a nearby bench, I'd read a few paragraphs and watch Tyler. Read, watch. Read, watch.

I wanted to keep him safe, of course. But I was also interested to see how Tyler interacted with other kids.

Which is why I can't shake the memory of the day, years ago, when I took Tyler to a park near my parents' retirement community in Florida. There was another young boy playing on a massive toy pirate ship. Tyler climbed aboard and started talking about animals. "Do you know the world's largest rodent? How about the smallest mammal? I saw a manatee . . ." His rapid-fire delivery caused his words and sentences to flow together. It was a muddle of minutiae that clearly irritated the other boy, who cupped his head in his hands and shouted, "My ears hurt!" Tyler continued jabbering. He didn't know why the boy ran away. I sure did.

I always had certain unrealistic notions of what Tyler would be. One of them was that he would be popular. You know, the boy whom other boys want to be *like*, and whom the girls want to be *with*. That moment in Florida—*My ears hurt!*—shook me to my core. I ached for my boy, of course, but also there was a selfish side of me. The side silently chastising Tyler for defying my expectations.

THE PECKING ORDER of childhood has roots in a social change that occurred about a century ago, when we started grouping kids in school by age. Until that time, most children were taught at home by their parents or a neighbor. Or they were grouped by school rather than by age—in small, one-room buildings staffed by teachers who educated children of all ages.

Before this shift, children developed self-esteem, social skills, and social mores with little input from age-equivalent peers. They modeled and learned from parents and other adults, largely independent of the competition and bad examples that modern-day children get from each other.

Perhaps the first empirical study on popularity among children appeared in the 1930s, when sociologists such as H. L. Koch and J. L. Moreno identified kids who were most liked and accepted by a majority of their peers. These "sociometric stars" shared a wide variety of positive attributes that would carry them through a lifetime of popularity and success, concluded early-20th-century experts on childhood.

For the next five or six decades, as parenting advice grew into an industry of magazines, books, and self-appointed gurus, a message freighted with pressure was drilled into parents: Popularity is good for your kids, and it's your job to help make them cool. The subtext: *You're only as successful as your child is popular.*

Toward the end of the 20th century, researchers started to question both the definition and the benefits of popularity. In a compilation of research called *Popularity in the Peer System*, the book's three editors cited a watershed study in which children were asked to list characteristics of popular kids. Researcher Antonius H. N. Cillessen expected to hear responses such as "kind," "funny," and "helps others out." While he did get some of that feedback, Cillessen also heard a surprising amount of negative responses, including "mean," "snobby," and "hurts other people."

Only recently, sociologists determined that "popularity" means something far different to them than it does to most children and parents. In simplest terms, sociologists study the *quality* of relationships, while parents sweat the *quantity*. Researchers focus their greatest attention on determining the depth and durability of friendships. They want to know how well a child knows the people closest to her or him, and how long the friendships might last. Is this a Facebook friend or a friend for life?

Parents are more superficial, which shouldn't be a surprise. We are not the experts, after all, and the actual experts told generations of parents that (a) popularity equals success and (b) good parents raise "sociometric stars." Both pieces of advice were wrong and destructive. Mothers and fathers learned to obsess over whether their kids are considered by their peers to be cool, and to measure popularity by the numbers. *How many boys came to Tyler's birthday party? How many girls came to Gabrielle's sleepover? How many playdates did Holly get invited to?*

I'll admit it: Lori and I counted our kids' friends. We yearned to see our children accepted by the so-called popular kids. We even lobbied the cool kids' parents: "Are you sure Heather can't come to Holly's party?"

After both Holly and Gabrielle graduated from college and moved out of state, Lori admitted that she had felt pressure to make our girls popular kids. "I was hoping they'd have friends and the social life I didn't have. I thought buying them things was the way to make that happen." Our baby girls wore designer clothes, and as they grew into teenagers their closets swelled with trendy styles. We drained our bank accounts for the hottest toys and electronic gadgets (I still maintain an unhealthy dislike for Cabbage Patch Kids). Lori pimped out our house for playdates, kept two refrigerators stocked with sodas, and had the pizza delivery numbers on speed dial. "I thought I could buy them friends."

I asked Tyler more than once, "How many friends

do you have at school?" This, too: "Why don't you invite them over to the house this weekend?" Inadvertently, my prodding signaled to Tyler that friendship is a concept so superficial that it can be quantified by numbers and defined by an afternoon in our basement. It was a dangerous message.

DESPITE ALL OUR efforts, Tyler was not a popular boy. The children who lived on our block had little patience for a marble-mouthed kid almost half their age who insisted—beyond almost any reasoning—that they all play by his rules. Their objections angered Tyler, and he didn't know how to control that emotion. He stomped and yelled, and he pushed the bigger kids.

One day, when I heard what was happening, I pulled Tyler aside and scolded him, just as I had done with his older sisters, and just as my father had done with me. Sternly I told him he couldn't behave that way and still expect to have friends. "I need you to apologize, Tyler. Tell them you're sorry." Showing no emotion, Tyler spun around and walked back to the kids. "Can we start over?" It wasn't an apology, and Tyler was impervious to the fact that his playmates were shaking their heads. But I remember chuckling to myself and thinking, *What a cute thing to say.*

Like his sisters and so many other millennials, Tyler was enthralled by Harry Potter books and movies.

Most kids develop affinities for the Hogwarts houses associated with intellect, courage, and ruthless ambition. Tyler considered himself a member of the Hufflepuff tribe, the most inclusive among the four houses, valued for hard work, patience, loyalty, and fair play. Hufflepuffs are kind and lighthearted underdogs. In the real world, they're most aptly compared to nerds or geeks. I asked Tyler once, "Why do you identify with the Hufflepuffs?"

He shrugged. "They are the ones nobody cares about."

It was worse in school, where even teachers shunned him. His preschool instructor complained about Tyler cracking jokes in class and said he was "too hyper and disorganized." She was right, but what struck me was her lack of empathy. "You seem very angry at my son," I told her. "Why is that?" We soon quit the school.

One of his first elementary school teachers, a well-meaning but overwhelmed public school veteran, could take only so much of Tyler's fidgeting, off-topic obsessions, and interruptions. In front of the class, she would tell him to put his head on his desk: "Take a nap." Ostracized, again.

WHY DO PARENTS crave popularity for their kids? In addition to decades of bad advice from the expert-industrial complex, there is the matter of our own egos. Stephen Gray Wallace, a school psychologist and president of the Center for Adolescent Research and Education (CARE), explained it to me this way: "We all want to be liked, right? On some level, we all want to be the coolest man or woman in the room. One way to do that in today's culture—as perverse as it sounds, as perverse as it *is*—is to raise a popular kid."

The "popular kids" are brilliant and funny and athletic and beautiful—endowed with the teenage mojo that makes their peers swoon while their moms and dads bask in the other parents' jealousy. "He's a chip off the old block." "That girl's got great genes."

Some parents are clear-eyed about yoking their self-esteem to their children's social status. Take John S., for example. The communications director at the attorney general's office in Michigan told me, "When we're at T-ball or baseball or football, I can tell that the other parents all do stuff together because their kids are together all the time. But they don't call us. They don't ask us to join them in whatever they're doing. When that happens, I feel a touch of 'I want that.'"

John is honest about his feelings and quietly owns them. I've seen other status-envy parents turn into graying versions of the petty blond social climbers featured in the 2004 movie *Mean Girls*. The ugliest example came one late October night, when I sat in the stands at a high school football game near our home and took notes on the conversations around me.

"This section is reserved for dance team parents," a father barked at me and a dozen other parents whose kids weren't members of the popular squad. We slouched away, like the scorned teenagers we hadn't been for three decades. In my new spot, I cradled a cup of coffee between my knees while listening to the conversation between two mothers in front of me. They were assessing the Yorktown High School homecoming court as several young couples strolled onto the field to take their bows.

"Can you believe what she's wearing?"

"Yes. She's a slut."

"Her date's going to play college ball."

"He doesn't have a brain in his gorgeous head."

It went on like this for 15 minutes, until one of the moms switched topics, bringing up her own son. "You know, it's not right that these kids are so damn happy and my Bobby can't make friends. It's not right."

Her friend nodded. The chatter stopped while the moms took sips from Styrofoam cups, the steam curling up toward me. "You're right. She's a slut."

POPULARITY IS A trap. The research is overwhelming. For instance, a study tracking nearly two hundred 13-year-olds over the course of a decade found that those who acted old for their age by sneaking into movies, forming early romantic relationships, shoplifting, and basing friendships on appearance were considered by their peers to be the popular kids. By the time the group turned 23, those same "popular kids" were significantly more likely to abuse drugs and break laws than their peers, and their behavior had backfired: Their peers no longer considered them cool.

This University of Virginia study, published by the journal *Child Development* in June 2014, found that the "cool" teens had a 45 percent greater rate of problems due to substance use by age 22, and a 22 percent greater rate of criminal behavior, compared with the average teen in the study. Such behavior made the popular group far less socially acceptable as young adults than they were at 13, which suggests that while the cool kids achieved temporary social status, they never developed the skills needed for deep, durable friendships. The shortcuts they took in middle school put them on a road to nowhere.

There is an insidious arc to popularity. It starts with teenagers' misbehaving to get into the popular crowd. Once they're on the A-list, popularity exposes them to other risk takers—peers who tempt them with sex, drugs, and criminal activity. They are then subjected to intense peer pressure, easily exploited by those who threaten banishment from the in-crowd.

Staying popular is a chore. You might recall the 1988 cult classic *Heathers*, a black comedy about the high school rivalries among popular girls, in which the lead character grimly complains that the other girls of her clique are "people I work with—and our job is being popular."

It should be no kid's job to be popular, said Wallace, the school psychologist and author who runs CARE. Wallace recalled a family friend, a boy whose immense popularity was due to his troublemaking. For instance, John (a pseudonym) was considered cool because he snuck booze from his parents' liquor cabinet and shared it with the other boys. By his early 20s, John was a heavy drinker. He eventually lost his job and his family, and he succumbed to alcoholism. "He just self-destructed," Wallace said. "It all started when he was a kid, when he was the cool kid."

There are better paths. We should stop pushing our kids to be popular, and encourage them to build friendships based on mutual interests, respect, and loyalty. Trust their instincts. Encourage them to follow their intuition, even if it doesn't match your expectations. Don't worry that your young teenager prefers to spend Saturday nights at home playing a video game, playing with you, or reading instead of going out with "friends."

Author Marybeth Hicks remembers joking in front of other mothers that her kids are geeks. "Oh, nooooo," one mom cooed. "You kids are very popular! Reeeally." The other mom seemed to think that raising popular children was Hicks' goal. "It's okay," Hicks explained. "We like that our kids are geeks."

In her book *Bringing Up Geeks*, Hicks encourages parents to pour their limited energies into raising genuine, enthusiastic, and empowered kids (she spins the attributes into the acronym GEEK). Writing about the anti-popularity parenting philosophy she shares with her husband, Hicks asked, "Are we sadistically imposing miserable childhoods on our four offspring for the sport of it? Heck no. We're simply committed to raising our children to have good characters and strong values. We are not raising them to be popular in elementary school and beyond. And the longer I'm a parent, the more I'm convinced these two goals often are mutually exclusive."

Hicks' approach reminds me of my father, an imposing Detroit motorcycle cop who quietly drilled five words into the heads of his four kids: "It's cool to be different." When the so-called popular kids tempted us to sneak a smoke or worse, Dad steeled us with the courage to proudly say no. *I'll pass. I'm different.* He didn't call us geeks, but I guess we were.

Joseph Allen, lead author on the University of Virginia study, told the *Los Angeles Times* there is a "quiet majority" of adolescents who are destined to be far more socially functional at an older age than their in-crowd peers. Tyler is part of the quiet majority of geekiness—and that's a good thing. While I stupidly, selfishly obsessed over the wrong expectations, he avoided the popularity trap.

WHILE WE FINISHED our coffee at the strip-mall Starbucks, I tried to explain to Stacey Bromberg how badly

I want Tyler to be popular. "If Lori and I could sculpt friends out of granite or program a few robotically, we would buy chisels and computer chips by the gross."

She smiled. "Me too." From the speaker above our heads, I heard a young man singing to his father. *Now it's just too late and we can't go back,* ended the Simple Plan anthem. *I'm sorry I can't be perfect.*

Bromberg told me about the day she volunteered at Gavin's school, stuffing folders with a group of fourth-graders. "One of the kids got to have a Lunch Bunch, which means he got to pick a couple of kids to eat a special lunch with. I watched this—I saw kids talking back and forth, laughing—and I started to cry," Stacey said. "A teacher asked me why I was crying, and I pointed to the kids laughing together and told her, 'My son doesn't do that.'"

One of my favorite bloggers is sportswriter Jeff Pearlman, who, while procrastinating on book projects, likes to reflect on his personal life. In 2014, he wrote about watching his fifth-grade daughter get razzed by classmates after a mediocre relay race. "Watching from about 20 yards away, I saw her face turn sad, but tried to stay out of things. As a parent, sometimes you need to let your child face hardship sans intervention. Then she approached and began to cry. Small tears that got a lot bigger. I gave her a hug . . . and that's when the magic happened."

A female classmate gave his daughter a hug and yelled, "Group hug!" Boys and girls engulfed her.

"Suddenly, at the same time her tears dried, mine formed," Pearlman wrote. "I was wearing sunglasses, so nobody noticed. But it was one of the most beautiful things I ever witnessed."

Beautiful because of what it says about his daughter and her peers. They are forming friendships with depth and durability. They are learning to stand up for each other—and stand against bad-acting peers. They are developing attributes of respect, compassion, and courage that will serve them well into adulthood. They are popular kids.

> Popularity is a good thing, but it is not
> something for which to sacrifice studies
> or athletic good standing in any way; and
> sometimes to seek it overmuch is to lose it.
>
> TEDDY ROOSEVELT, IN A LETTER TO
> TED JUNIOR, OCTOBER 11, 1905

4

SUPERSTAR

"My Kid Was a Great Player . . ."

Grand Rapids, Michigan—*Dad looks old. Just a year ago, he was lifting his weight and walking the treadmill at the gym every day. But now he shuffles his feet and slouches, his once ramrod posture diminished and shaped like an S. Today he's transfixed by the past—specifically, he's staring at a life-sized, black-and-white photograph of Detroit riot police clashing with angry protesters. Tyler and I are in Grand Rapids to tour the Gerald R. Ford Presidential Museum. We're also visiting my parents, who moved here after giving Florida a brief tryout.*

Dad retired from the Detroit Police Department in 1986, ending a career that defined him and included two decades in a motorcycle unit that doubled as a riot squad. "I was just talking to your mom about those days," *Dad says. He lifts a heavy hand and points to the riot picture at the center of the*

1960s exhibit. "We fought in the bad neighborhoods, all the while wondering whether the bad guys were burning down our homes, too. It was so close but so far away." The rioting occurred several miles from a street in northeast Detroit called Coram, a tidy block of middle-class homes where Mom and Dad both grew up, fell in love, raised four kids, and eased their own parents into retirement and death.

Coram also is where my dad taught me how to hit and throw a ball. How to ride a bike and drive a car. How to avoid a fight when you can, and win a fight when you can't avoid it. How to compete hard, succeed with humility, and never get accustomed to losing. Shortly after I brought Lori home to Coram for the first time, Dad shared his two secrets to marriage. "First, even when she's wrong," he told me, "she's right." Dad flashed his wry smile, the one Mom calls a shit-eating grin. "Second, always put her first. As much as I loved you kids, I never forgot that you would grow up and be gone, and I'd always be with your mom."

As we walk through the Ford museum, I wonder how long he'll be with Mom. Dad has neuropathy, nerve damage that has cost him feeling in his feet, but my siblings and I suspect our parents are hiding something worse. Before leaving for the museum today, over breakfast at my parents' apartment, I had expressed my concerns to both Mom and Dad. They confirmed that he was sick—but only indirectly and vaguely. "I may need to have somebody drive me around the rest of my life," Dad said.

Mom insisted, "Everything's fine, honey." She was talk-

ing to Dad, not me. Later she told me to stop prying. "Let your dad feel a little bit in control."

"WHAT'S WRONG WITH you, Bompa?"

Tyler's question snaps me back to the present—and I see why Tyler is alarmed. His grandfather is swaying slighting, gingerly grabbing the curved metal frame around the Detroit riot picture.

"I'm okay, pal," Dad mumbles. "Let's look around more." He points toward a chunk of the Berlin Wall in a Cold War exhibit. Tyler fires off a series of facts and anecdotes about the Cold War, something about Stalin and East Germany, an airlift, and "President Ford's blunder about Poland."

Dad smiles. "He's like a little professor."

The next stop is a replica of the Oval Office, where Tyler stands and stares—remembering the visit nearly 10 years earlier. Tyler points to a door, the one disguised as part of the wall, through which we had walked in to see Bush. "I'm not going to get back in, am I?" he asks.

"Maybe," I reply. "As president."

"If so," Tyler says, "I'm bringing my dog, Rascal."

We tour the Watergate exhibit, which bluntly recounts the crimes of the Nixon administration. Tyler recognizes the site of the infamous burglary of the Democratic National Committee headquarters as the place where I now work, the Watergate complex. I try to slip a morality lesson into the tour. "So you know," I tell Tyler, "President Ford tried to help the country heal by pardoning Richard Nixon. What does that tell you about real life?"

Without hesitation, he says, "You do lot of good things and you do one bad thing and people don't forgive you."

Ford was a father of four children who mostly avoided the pitfalls of other presidential kids. His father, Leslie King, was a brute—an alcoholic who reportedly beat Ford's mother on the couple's honeymoon. She had smiled at another man. The future president was still an infant when his parents divorced, and his mother eventually married Gerald Rudolff Ford, who raised and inspired the budding athlete.

I don't see a museum display on fatherhood. But there is a glass case filled with a football helmet, jersey, and other mementos of Ford's athletic prowess at the University of Michigan. It triggered memories: I had played organized football through middle school, and Dad had tried to talk me into trying out for the high school team; my only regret from childhood was that I didn't listen.

"I hated to see you stop playing," Dad says. My stomach tightens. I let Dad down?

Tyler breaks the awkward silence. "Why do you make me play football, Dad?" Tyler plays flag football.

I tell him, "Me and Mom think it's good for you."

"I disagree," he says.

Dad grins, nods to his grandson, and tells me, "Maybe you should listen." I give Dad a curious look. He thought I should try out for football. I ran cross-country instead and al-

ways assumed that Dad disapproved. He says no. "You might regret it now, but cross-country was good for you," Dad says, "and I'll never regret not pushing you."

For the first time I tell Dad why I quit football: As I prepared to enter eighth grade, a federal court approved the Detroit Public School desegregation plan that would require me and my siblings to ride buses across town to a mostly black neighborhood. My parents opposed busing—they considered it social experimentation, with their kids as guinea pigs—and so they enrolled us in the affluent Grosse Pointe school district. I felt like I didn't belong, because I didn't. We still lived in Detroit, a violation of Grosse Pointe policy that we had to keep secret, and my classmates were far richer than a cop's kid. I tell Dad: I was insecure and alone and essentially living a lie. I didn't want to try out for a football team I might not make. I was afraid of failure.

"I know," Dad says. "You got over it. You haven't been scared by much since." Grandfather, son, and grandson stare at Ford's soft leather helmet until Dad breaks the silence. "You're not me," he says, nodding at Tyler, "and he's not you."

CLUMPED LIKE ANTS around the last crumb at a picnic, two sets of 6-year-olds—half dressed in red shirts and shorts, half in pale blue—vibrated around a frayed soccer ball, kicking it, swatting it, and in one case spitting at it. "Spread out! Spread out!" shouted Mary Schade, a part-time tutor and former teacher who turned to soccer coaching after raising her own kids. "Dearies," she chuckled, "would you please mind spreading out?"

Clutching coffee mugs and paper Starbucks cups, a couple dozen parents organized themselves into groups: The Bored, happily delegating authority to Coach Schade while thumbing newspapers, scanning smartphones, and scratching yellow highlighters through books and legal briefs; The Adoring, mothers and a few fathers cheering each other's kids in a community of adulation; and The Great Santinis, mostly dads and one mom yelling instructions and rebukes. The one drill-sergeant mom shrieked, "Get your finger out of your nose, Danny, and spread out!"

The knot of boys and girls moved in unison, a multicellular colony organized around its grass-stained nucleus, until one cell split from the rest and wandered off. It was Tyler. Taking his eye off the ball and his mind off the game, my son scooted 15 yards from the pack with stiff-legged strides. "What's he doing?" I asked Lori. Noticing an edge in my voice, she shot me an annoyed look.

"Maybe's he's looking for a pass," Lori said.

"Heck of a way to get a pass," I scoffed.

Tyler bent his knees, fell on his butt, and plucked a dandelion from midfield. "Stand up, Tyler!" shouted the coach. Tyler smiled, puckered his lips, and blew a small cloud of seeds across the soccer pitch. Then he caught my eye and waved. "Hi, Dad!" I waved and grimaced, the tortured body language of a dad trying to simultaneously say *Love you* and *Get your ass back in the game*.

PARENTS TODAY ENCOURAGE, guide, nudge, push, and force their kids into all forms of organized activities. Sports, of course. But there's a broad bouquet of parental aspirations: science fairs, spelling bees, singing contests, class elections, beauty pageants, bake-offs, ballet, and more. We want them to be stars, most valuable of *something*. You say my Johnny can't play shortstop? Maybe he can play the guitar! Brenda's singing voice is a bit pitchy? Let's see if she can pitch! We love our kids and want the best for them, so why not help them *be* the best? Any advantage is a good thing, right?

That's what Elizabeth S. told me in a pale pink hallway at BalletNova, a dance studio in Falls Church, Virginia. Wearing tight jeans and an off-the-shoulders black fringed top, Elizabeth had the chiseled face and frame of a dancer. "I performed my whole life up until I had kids, almost went professional," said the corporate secretary and single mother from Washington, D.C. "That's why I bring her here." Elizabeth nodded at Angel. "I just want her to be a happy little girl."

For parents like Elizabeth, not just any organized activity will do. *Be like me*, they tell their kids—or *Be what I hoped to be.* Angel was not happy. She was sniffing back tears and rubbing her eyes, whispering to her mom, "I don't want to go. I don't want to go."

Elizabeth dismissed her protests. "I know you're not crazy about it now," she told the girl, "but Mommy didn't like dancing at first, either."

I asked Elizabeth about her daughter's true passion—maybe sports? She wrinkled her nose in disgust. "I know it's not PC for me to say, but I want her to be a little girl. I want her to marry a nice guy—to be swept off her feet and be a mom. First I want her to be a dancer. It's a glorious life," she said.

The studio door opened with a thud, and the narrow hallway was assaulted by two dozen 4-year-olds in pink tutus. "I did it!" one of them yelled while running into her mother's arms. "How'd you do?" a father asked another. Almost lost in the torrent of noisy reunions, Angel lifted her head from Elizabeth's shoulder and said again, "I don't want to go."

"Go now," Elizabeth said, stroking the girl's cornrows. "Have fun."

Watching Angel slouch into the studio made me think of something written by David Brooks, a *New York Times* columnist with a keen eye for social change. He said "an epidemic of conditional love" is shaping parenting early in the 21st century. "Many parents bestow or withdraw their affection depending on how well their children are achieving, producing millions of young people without secure emotional foundations, who pine for any kind of approval." The mother of four who wrote the book about geeks, Marybeth Hicks, said children are not just family for many parents, they're an accomplishment. They're trophies.

Many mothers and fathers (yes, including me) trumpet their children's success in school, sports, the arts, and the entire gamut of activities that allow for ranking—kid vs. kid and parent vs. parent. It's a lot for a child to bear.

THE PEOPLE WE hire to sculpt and shine our tiny trophies often make matters worse. Coaches who curse their players, bully them to play through injuries, and preach teamwork while keeping hardworking players on the bench. Pageant and contest organizers who profit off the competitions, recruiting kids with false expectations to pile up entrance fees. Teachers and tutors who ruthlessly weed out average and below-average students in search of the prodigy.

Average no longer is good enough, particularly in sports, where professionalism has encroached on puberty—for both girls and boys. One coach, Randel Hanson, wrote in *Commons* magazine with author Kathryn Milun, "For youth baseball, this professionalization often means playing year-round on hyper-competitive and exclusive club teams for as many as

120-plus games annually, regularly traveling to interstate and even international tournaments, teaching kids to throw curve balls at ever younger ages, and demanding time commitments which rival that of Major League Baseball participants."

This intensity twists the concept of sportsmanship. One in every 10 kids acknowledged cheating in a game, according to a 2005 study published in the *Journal of Research in Character Education*, while 13 percent had tried to hurt an opponent. Twenty percent of coaches reportedly made fun of kids on their teams.

One of the largest U.S. coalitions of professional and amateur sports organizations, Citizens Through Sports Alliance, finds youth sports lacking in emotional support. With input from parents, coaches, officials, and program directors, the group's 2005 report card gave average grades to coaching and officiating. Two categories received D's: "child-centered philosophy" and "parental behavior."

Every 25 seconds in America, a child visits an emergency room for a sports-related injury, according to a Safe Kids Worldwide survey, for a total of 1.35 million children in 2012 alone. The figures don't include injuries due to "overuse," 25 percent of which are serious. In a *New York Times* op-ed column, pediatric orthopedic surgeon Ron J. Turker recalled an office visit by a teenager named Lucas and his two parents. He told them Lucas had a torn anterior cruciate ligament.

"You don't understand, this is his life!" the boy's mom said.

"We need this fixed—he's in the Olympic Development Program!" the dad said of his 13-year-old son. "He's elite!"

MOST PARENTS KNOW the drill. We toggle between competing emotions: disappointment when our kids don't conquer an activity; pride when they do; and gnawing guilt for raising them, selfishly and destructively, as extensions of our dreams. The parents most buffeted by these feelings are those who imagined their child as a mini-me.

An acquaintance of mine named Fergus Cullen is a competitive distance runner who has coached high school teams for 15 years. As much as he adores his 9-year-old son, Jacob, Cullen said there was no getting around the fact that "Jacob is not like me." The boy struggled in school and had no taste for sports. One year, Cullen was visiting his parents' home when his nephew walked into the living room and asked permission to watch ESPN, the sports network. A wave of shame crashed over Cullen as he said to himself, *Gosh, I love to watch a little* SportsCenter *with my nephew, but that's never going to happen with Jacob.*

For many parents, like Cullen, the basic desire to bond with their children compels them to push.

In simpler times, a parent and child bonded through work—on the farm or on behalf of the family. The relationship wasn't ideal, but it was reliable. Modern parents compete with new technology and new media not just for their kids' time and attention but also for their *interests*. "If I can't convince him to play catch with me," said Cullen, who works in New Hampshire as a political consultant, "I know darn well I'm going to lose him to the screens."

David B. is a Wall Street broker who lives in New Jersey with his wife and two kids. When his son, Richard, threatened to quit baseball during middle school, David balked. He told me, "My kid was a great player, and to just give it up . . ."

David's wife told her husband to ease off: "You're always trying to put baggage on him." David found comfort in an episode of the ABC comedy *Modern Family*, one where the father freaks out because his young son suddenly asks to stop performing magic, their shared passion. That dad at first refuses to listen. "This isn't about magic," he says.

"No," replies the son. "It's about my life and you controlling it."

The follow-in-my-footsteps fantasy is just one reason for the professionalization of childhood. Another is economic pressure, which increases the appeal for prize money, fattened college applications and scholarships, and pro contracts. The new economy also has increased the number of two-income families, which means kids today are without parental supervision more than ever. After-school clubs, academic tutors, organized athletics, and the like are competition-cum-babysitting.

In the summer, with school out, busy parents pay small fortunes to enroll their kids in "camps." Not that long ago, summer camp consisted of rustic cabins, bonfires, lakes, and woods—everybody thrown together and thrown outdoors. Today, summer camp can be indoors and gravitate toward one of two extremes: maniacally competitive (my niece attends piano camp for budding prodigies) or structured to pander to teen trends and tastes. One year, Tyler attended a two-week camp at a boarding school in Connecticut where he studied the history of the world via video games.

PAST GENERATIONS OF parents had more realistic expectations—lower and less ambitious—than today's moms and dads. It was understood that an unlucky number of children are born disabled, a fortunate few become superstars in some field, and most of us are perfectly middling. That used to be okay. But modern parents don't always accept those odds. We'd rather define the extraordinary downward by pretending that everybody is a winner. It's the superstar syndrome. From the playing fields to the recital halls and beyond, every parent's "trophy" gets a trophy.

Children aren't dummies. They know there's a cost

for the affirmation and ambition. "The only way to pay back parents for their sacrifices and efforts is through accomplishments, be they academic, athletic, or social," write Dr. Alvin Rosenthal and Nicole Wise in *The Overscheduled Child*. This principle applies not just to sports but also to the variety of ways modern parents enmesh themselves in the lives of their children. Kids face two sorts of pressure from moms and dads: the kind that comes in their parents' direct pursuit of achievement, and the indirect pressure that children intuitively absorb.

Some kids crack. One of every five 18-year-olds has suffered major depression, and nearly 9 percent of adolescents have been diagnosed with an anxiety disorder. *The Overscheduled Child* authors, one of whom is a child psychiatrist, attribute those numbers largely to pressures from mothers and fathers. While others may disagree, the consensus of experts is that the rise of depression and anxiety is strongly linked to parental expectations.

More than a dozen years ago, David Brooks wrote a seminal essay in *The Atlantic* titled "The Organization Kid," decrying what he called America's "achievement ethos" and the result: a generation of children leading a "frenetic, tightly packed existence." Kids want their childhood back. Nearly 80 percent of American children say they wish they had more free time, according to a 2006 survey conducted by the KidsHealth

KidsPoll, while 41 percent say they feel stressed most of the time because they have too much to do.

When today's parents were growing up, kids wandered the neighborhood. Curb ball, hide-and-seek, kick the can, king of the hill, cowboys and Indians, footraces, bike races, sack races, and long treks to the store, paper-route money crumpled in sweaty pockets. Sports were mostly played pickup—"shirts vs. skins and Mr. Briggs' house is an automatic out!" Organized sports involved a game on the weekends and a few weekday practices, but still there was plenty of time to *just play.*

We overschedule our kids, enable their digital distractions, and shield them from harm—and the result is what experts call a national "play crisis." Seventy percent of mothers say they played outdoors every day when they were young, according to a study by Rhonda Clements of Manhattanville College, compared with only 31 percent of their children. Recess time has been trimmed or cut in schools across the country. The National Institute for Play (NIP) estimates that playtime outside has decreased 71 percent in one generation in both the United States and the United Kingdom.

Scientists say that when children play, neurons fire in a child's prefrontal cortex, where executive functions are controlled. That makes play critical to learning how to control emotions, make plans, and solve problems. "Whether it's rough-and-tumble play or two kids deciding to build a sand castle together, the kids themselves have to negotiate, 'Well, what are we going to do in this game? What are the rules we are going to follow?'" Sergio Pellis, a researcher at the University of Lethbridge in Alberta, Canada, told National Public Radio for a series on kids' play. And after years of researching violent individuals, the NIP concluded that play actually can deter violence in children.

Nobody is suggesting that your kids will become ax murderers unless you loosen the reins on play. But give it a try. Your children stand a better chance of being socially connected and successful adults if you ease off the structure, loosen up on the rules, and, whenever possible, simply let them play.

Just chill. Odds are high that your children will never be truly exceptional in any field. Guaranteed: Your children will be godawful in more endeavors than not. In most ways, on most days, for most kids, much of their lives will be spent within spitting distance of mediocrity. Average Joes and Janes. We should refashion parenthood by tolerating pain, play, and failure. We should measure our children not by the mountains they conquer but by their efforts to climb.

Oh—and let them pick which hills to scale.

THE DAY WE learned our third child would be our first boy, Lori panicked. She knew how to raise girls and was busy with two of them. But a boy? "I don't even know how to get his hair cut," she gasped. But I knew what to do. I bought him a baseball glove.

The tiny plastic mitt was designed for show, not for shortstops—the perfect trophy for his nursery of my dreams. A blue-and-orange blanket with the Detroit Tigers' Old English *D* covered one wall. Hockey jerseys autographed by Red Wings legends hung from three others. Atop a shelf painted with tiger stripes, next to a complete set of 1997 baseball cards and a framed picture of Hall of Famer Ty Cobb, sat a diary I kept for my son. We nicknamed him "Ty" and "Tiger." One night when he was 2 months old, I rocked him to sleep while writing in a diary about the "perfect day" we had just spent together.

"I tucked you in my right arm and munched on a cheese ball with my left hand while our favorite team, the Detroit Lions, beat the Jets to get into the playoffs," I wrote in the soft glow of a baseball-shaped night-light. "Barry Sanders gained his 2,000th yard of the year and, while I jumped out of my seat with you in my arms, yelling and twirling both of us around, your eyes popped wide open." Looking ahead, I wrote: "I hope we share lots of time together. It doesn't have to be football or any other sport, just as long as you're happy and proud to be with your dad."

What a load of crap. Those last two sentences are a lie, family fiction—the first draft of my fairy tale on fatherhood. The truth: Eighteen years ago, I couldn't imagine Tyler being happy, or me being proud, *without* sports. The machine of American mythology had told me so: Sports are the glue that binds generations of fathers and sons from cradle to grave, as famously illustrated in the movie *Field of Dreams*. "Hey, Dad," the Iowa farmer said to his father's ghost. "You wanna have a catch?" For other parents, the field of dreams might be a Broadway stage, an operating table, or a courtroom—but their hopes are just as big and often beyond reach.

Most boys idolize their fathers, but I might have taken hero worship a step beyond the norm. My dad had a habit of blinking fast and hard when he was nervous, clenching his eyes like tiny fists. I did, too—an odd quirk for a happy 5-year-old. Dad pulled absentmindedly at his T-shirt, twisting dirty wrinkles into the white fabric bunched at his midsection. Mom would see me do the same, and she'd ask, "You got a tummyache?" Dad jerked his shoulders every few strides, like a football player adjusting his shoulder pads. I still do that. Dad's enormous gait came with a slight limp, the result of a knee-crushing car wreck in the mid-1960s. Lori says I carry the same ponderous stride into my fifth decade.

"When you walk away," my wife told me at my parents' 50th-anniversary party, "you look just like your dad." The comparison made me smile, and I wondered, *Will Tyler be like me?*

My dad was fiercely competitive. He counted cards

like a euchre savant and expected that his kids would do the same. He adored his mother-in-law for many reasons, not the least of which was Granny's no-prisoners approach to games. They loved playing together, though a stranger wouldn't recognize the joy in their cussing, complaining, and cheating. Yes, cheating: In our house, when it came to family games, *finesse* was a synonym for the dark arts. Dad and Granny would warn visitors that if you're not watching your cards, you deserve what you get. Neither of them would ease up, much less throw a game, even when teaching us kids how to play. That competitive fire helped me as a journalist, as I suspect it kept Dad safe on the streets.

One of Dad's favorite assignments as a cop was directing traffic at Red Wings hockey games. He often brought me and my brothers, Tim and Mike, to the stadium, where the locker room attendant kept an eye on us while Dad worked. We were rink rats, and we got to know Dad's childhood hero, Hall of Famer Gordie Howe, as he was winding down his career. Years later, on a family visit to Traverse City, Michigan, Dad drove past Howe's house and saw the legend cutting his own lawn. We had to stop him from bolting out of the car to help "Mr. Howe."

Fathers and sons don't always know how to talk to each other, which is why we have sports. I never felt closer to my dad than when we played catch. He didn't believe as much in saying "I love you" as he did in showing it, and sports were one way he knew how.

And so, from the moment Tyler could cock his arm, I put a ball at the end of it. On September 19, 1999, when Tyler was not quite 2, I wrote about our first game of catch. "You scrambled up the small slope of a neighbor's front yard and sat down, facing me. I showed you how to hold your tiny hands out, palms up. When I threw the fuzzy yellow tennis ball it hit your hands and rolled into your lap." I pronounced that his first catch.

Year after year, I dragged Tyler outside with a baseball, football, basketball, volleyball, hockey stick, badminton racquet, or croquet mallet. I signed him up for Babe Ruth baseball, flag football, and hockey lessons. He was awful at all of them. He never wanted to play.

One time he played catcher (my old position!) for a Little League team of 8- and 9-year-olds. With every pitch, I stood behind home plate, my fingers gripping the wire-mesh backstop, as Tyler waved at the ball. Each pitch sailed over his shoulder or bounced at his feet, striking the umpire with a thud—followed by a grunt from the ump and, occasionally, a whispered curse. "Catch the ball, buddy. Block the ball, buddy." I repeated the refrain for three innings, until the coach pulled Tyler out of the game and sat him on the bench.

The bench is the last place a ballplayer wants to be. Tyler called the bench his "happy place."

There was no happiness for Tyler on a basketball court, either. I remember one excruciating game he spent at half-court, sprinting back and forth a few feet either side of the center line. His stiff, awkward strides were no match for the other nine boys, who blew past him in their full-court dashes, looking comparably feline. At one point Tyler looked up at me in the stands, shrugged, lifted his palms toward the ceiling, and shot me a bemused smile, as if to say, *This ain't for me.*

I never got mad, but I wouldn't give in. First, Lori and I believed, Tyler needed the exercise. Second, he needed to learn what it means to be part of a team, particularly after we started to notice that he was strangely isolated from his peers. Tyler knew I wanted him to be a jock. But after a half dozen years of butting heads about sports, he had come to hate them—and he hated that I pushed.

I STOPPED PUSHING when my father reminded me at the Ford library that he'd never pushed me. *You're not me and he's not you.* It was clear what I had to do; the only question was how. Lori, of course, had the answer. When Tyler and I returned home from the Michigan trip, she said that I should cut a deal with him: Tyler could quit sports if he promised to exercise regularly and join an extracurricular club in school.

I sat him down in the living room and offered him the bargain. "What do you think, bud?"

Tyler smiled. "You got a deal." He shook my hand, then grew quiet.

I asked, "What's wrong?"

He said, "I was afraid you wouldn't like me as much if I stopped playing sports."

> A carefree, well-to-do man who didn't
> really give a damn about the hopes
> and dreams of his firstborn son.
>
> GERALD R. FORD, DESCRIBING HIS BIOLOGICAL
> FATHER, IN HIS 1979 MEMOIR, *A TIME TO HEAL*

5

SUCCESSFUL

"She Can't Wait to Tell Her Friends, 'Oh, My Daughter Goes to Harvard. I'm Such a Great Parent'"

Boston, Massachusetts—*What a frustrating kid. I can't get him to talk to me, and when I do, it's one or two words and a grunt. Tyler and I are touring the John F. Kennedy Library and Presidential Museum today, and he's driving me nuts.*

"What was your favorite thing about the other day?" I ask.

"The end," he says.

It was a softball question about the trip to nearby Quincy, Massachusetts, where we had toured the homestead of the first father-son presidents. Today my plan is to explore the complicated relationship between JFK and his father, Joseph Kennedy Sr., a domineering dad who wanted his eldest son, Joe junior, to become president. After Joe junior's death during World War II, JFK became the target of his father's obsession.

Now I'm obsessed with getting Tyler to talk about his

future—his career. But those are things he doesn't like to talk about, especially when his attention-deficit issues get him revving. He's frantic, flitting between exhibits like a moth against a well-lit window. He's also hilarious.

The Briefing Room: "Dude had a funny accent."

The Campaign Trail: "Did you cover this election, Dad? You're old enough."

The Space Race: "We won."

The Oval Office: "No dog in this one!"

While Tyler runs ahead, I linger over the family exhibit, where the mythology of Kennedy's destiny is encased in glass. Artifact after artifact reflects the weight of paternal expectations: Kathleen Kennedy's Red Cross uniform jacket, a blackthorn walking stick, and something called a "Kennedy family commemorative cup." JFK had to contend with the legacy of two powerful Boston clans: the Fitzgeralds and the Kennedys.

"When my great grandfather left here to become a cooper in East Boston, he carried nothing with him except two things: a strong religious faith and a strong desire for liberty," the exhibit quotes Kennedy as saying on a trip to Ireland a few months before his assassination. "I am glad to say that all of his great grandchildren have valued that inheritance."

I catch up with Tyler and try again. "Ty, I'm not joking. What was your favorite thing about the other day?"

He chuckles. "The beginning."

"Dammit, son. What was your favorite thing?"

"The trolley ride, because it came at the beginning and the end."

He laughs while I try to bury my anger. Lori tells me all

the time: I can't teach Tyler how to hold a conversation if I can't hold my emotions.

"Everything is not a joke," I say calmly. "Look at my face, son. My face is telling you that you're hurting my feelings when you joke about something that's serious to me."

"I don't know how to read faces," Tyler says. He's messing with me.

"That's why we're here, Ty. That's why Mom sent us on these trips. You need to read faces."

He's learned to read one face, at least—mine—and is taking full advantage. I look at him and take a deep breath, silently counting to five. "So what was your favorite thing about the other day?"

"The end, I said." He laughs.

THE DOOR SLAMMED behind me, shutting out the sunny Saturday afternoon and sucking me into a vibrating vortex of noise: squealing kids, clanging bells, and one muffled, overamplified baritone: "Kim! . . . Kim! . . . party of Kim!" Adjusting my eyes to the dark lobby of Ultrazone Laser Tag in Falls Church, Virginia, I saw a microphone in the hand of a craggy-faced teenage boy. "Birthday party of Kim!" he announced, swiping dirty bangs from his eyes. "Room 6, please."

Behind him were six party rooms, glorified closets crammed with two types of humanity: sugar-buzzed children and their parents. The kids had taken over, vacuuming ginormous amounts of pizza, ice cream, and sheet cake into their mouths when they weren't pouring tokens into video machines, wrestling on stained carpets, or waiting in a ragged line to enter the laser tag course. For those not indoctrinated, a typical game of laser tag unleashes two teams of kids into a dark room to climb and crawl through a maze of obstacles while shooting each other with light-pulsing guns hooked electronically to what kids call "kill sensors," which are placed over their dark little hearts. In other words, it's insane.

Because it was a typical weekend afternoon, the children outnumbered adults roughly 10 to 1, and it showed in the parents' eyes. Experienced mothers and fathers had bored, vacant stares: *Been here, done this.* New parents looked wide-eyed and terrified: *Why am I here?* The answer is, because you love your children. One way you show that love these days is by shoveling money at customized, commercialized birthday parties in places like Ultrazone Laser Tag.

I was there to test a theory: Birthdays serve a purpose known only to parents. More than an expression of love and a marking of time, they're annual checkups. Expectations Celebrations. They give moms and dads a chance to take stock of their progeny—to measure their kids' progress against their goals for them. Uncles, aunts, grandparents, and other family members gather to eat cake and sing "Happy Birthday" before sending the kids off to play so they can brag and bitch about the little ones. The birthday boy (or girl) gets the most thorough social colonoscopy (*Are his grades any better than last year? Did she make the travel team this year?*), but soon the adults are comparing each other's kids.

Our neighborhood in suburban Washington is a cradle of type A parents—affluent, mostly white social climbers who want the "right kids" at their kids' birthday parties for the same reason they jockey to attend the A-list dinner parties: status. A father once bragged to me about how a moon-bounce rental had "paid off big-time" because the children of two congressmen and a cable television pundit attended TJ's birthday bash.

I had lunch recently with a well-regarded business consultant, a mother and wife with two young kids—one boy, one girl. This woman, one of five sisters in a large southern family, long dreamed of raising a daughter in her image. As she put it: "A girly girl—you know, a sweet and loving little thing who might have a career and all, but she'd always be a lady." My friend rushed through lunch because she had to buy decorations for her daughter's 9th-birthday party. "You know what the theme is? *Star Trek*," she said, laughing herself red in the face. "My girly girl wants a *Star Trek*–themed 9th-birthday party."

Will she get it? "Of course," the mother replied, "but I do hope this is just a nerdy stage that wears off."

In less-entitled neighborhoods, birthday parties

tend to be as pragmatic as the parents' ambitions. Jhakeye Garcia is a first-generation American from Bolivia, a single mother of two children who lives in a blue-collar neighborhood outside Washington. She wants her kids to stay out of trouble and in school, and to climb past her on the socioeconomic ladder. "Our birthday parties are pretty simple," she told me. "A few friends, a cake, and some of those traditional games— you know, like pin the tail on the donkey." I nodded. She had just described the quintessential birthday party of the 1950s and 1960s, before extravagance became the norm in neighborhoods like mine.

WHEN I WANDERED into Room 6 at Ultrazone, I found three mothers sitting at a table littered with sticky cake plates, pizza boxes, and cups. Their boys were on the laser tag course, and they agreed to talk to me about the future they hoped their kids would have. "Good marks," declared Mrs. Kim, the mother of the birthday boy. "Good marks . . . and I want him to grow up to be a good person."

I rolled my eyes. The women giggled. "That's the answer I'm supposed to give," Mrs. Kim said.

"I'll tell you the truth," interrupted her friend Connie O. "My son wants to be an artist. He loves drawing and is really into music. I want him to be a neurosurgeon." Her friends nodded. Career choice is a point of dispute already between these moms and their 12-year-olds.

"Just the thought of him doing something that's not with his mind, that doesn't involve some mental achievement, really bothers me," Connie said.

I asked why.

"Because of who we are," she said. "You know."

No, I didn't know.

"Because we're Asian," answered the third woman, Eve G.

"We're tiger moms," Connie chuckled. A first-generation American, Connie considers herself fully assimilated but barely clinging to the middle class. "I know it's not politically correct, but intellectual and career status means a lot to Asian parents. There's a lot of pressure on our kids to succeed in this world, and a lot of pressure on us to make them succeed. And I'll tell you this . . . ."

Pulling a plastic fork out of her son's half-eaten cake, Connie swept a gob of white icing into her mouth and closed her eyes. She gathered her thoughts before sharing them, speaking slowly for emphasis. "My . . . precious . . . little . . . boy . . . is going to be . . . a god-damned neurosurgeon."

THE CONSUMMATION OF all parental expectations are the aspirations tied to adulthood—what career paths our kids will take, what kind of people they'll marry, where and how they'll live, and how many grandchildren they'll give us. Often when we ask our children, "What do you want to be when you grow up?" we're actually telling them, *This is what I want you to be.*

In 1930, behavioral psychologist John B. Watson said, "Give me a dozen healthy infants, well-formed, and my own specified world to bring them up in and I'll guarantee to take any one at random and train him to become any type of specialist I might select—doctor, lawyer, artist, merchant-chief and, yes, even beggar-man and thief, regardless of his talents, penchants, tendencies, abilities, vocations, and race of his ancestors." Watson considered children to be balls of clay that parents can mold for life. He was wrong. Children are more like foam balls. They yield easily to pressure, but once the pressure is released, they return to form. Unrelenting pressure can crush them.

Modern child behaviorists are united in the belief that parents should embrace the fact that a child's future depends chiefly on the child. Focus on the moment, build a loving relationship, and redefine the perfect outcome. Don't limit yourself to standard measures of a child's success, such as grades, trophies, and acceptance letters from elite preschools and graduate schools. And don't swaddle your kids in praise and privilege.

Psychologist and bestselling author Madeline Levine upended conventional wisdom by showing that children from affluent families are experiencing depression, anxiety, psychosomatic disorders, and substance abuse at higher rates than kids from poor families. Privileged kids also are more likely to develop stress, exhaustion, depression, anxiety, an unhealthy reliance on others for support, and a poor sense of self. Their coping mechanisms often include substance abuse, self-mutilation, and sex. "The cost of this relentless drive to perform at unrealistically high levels is a generation of kids who resemble nothing so much as trauma victims," she wrote in *Teach Your Children Well*.

You might think you're avoiding this trap by praising your kids—telling them they're the smartest, funniest, and best-looking of all children—or by shielding them from failure and responsibility. You would be wrong. Praise begets pressure. And it can be counterproductive.

In a typical experiment, researchers at Stanford University asked young children to solve a simple puzzle. Then they told some of the kids how smart and successful they are. The rest of the kids got no feedback. The children without praise were more motivated to solve increasingly difficult puzzles. They also exhibited higher levels of confidence and made significantly more progress on the puzzles than the group smothered in praise. "Praising children's talents and abilities seems to rattle their confidence," Levine wrote in a *New York Times* story summarizing the research by

Carol Dweck. "Tackling more difficult puzzles carries the risk of losing one's status as 'smart' and deprives kids of the thrill of choosing to work simply for its own sake, regardless of outcomes."

The best approach, according to decades of studies, is to be what child development experts call an "authoritative parent." These mothers and fathers are involved and responsive. They set high expectations but respect their kids' autonomy. They are the Goldilocks of parenting—not too hard (clinically defined as "authoritarian") or too soft ("permissive")—and they tend to raise children who do better academically, psychologically, and socially than their peers.

The children of Goldilocks parents don't get trophies just for showing up. They're allowed to fail. A Goldilocks mother would never declare, "You're going to an Ivy League school," nor would she shrug and say, "I don't care if you go to college." A Goldilocks father doesn't second-guess his daughter's academic and career choices, doesn't push his son into sports, and doesn't fret over his daughter's choice for a husband.

I was no Goldilocks parent.

OUR ELDEST CHILD, Holly, studied anthropology at James Madison University. Yes, anthropology—and it drove me nuts, because as I kept telling her, there are no jobs in anthropology. "Why do you want to be poor for a living?" I asked. This makes me fairly typical, according to Cynthia Edwards, the psychology professor in Raleigh, North Carolina. "This crowd of students is coming of age in a time of tremendous economic tumult. That would be bad enough for them," she told me. "But they're also dealing with hand-wringing parents."

When Holly graduated, I urged her to enroll in City Year, a program that places young adults in big cities, where, for a small stipend and graduate-school tuition, they do public service. Born in Arkansas and raised in suburban Washington, Holly asked to serve in Detroit—a city she had visited three or four times a year while growing up, because Lori and I were determined to remain connected to our families and to the Midwest. Holly's first apartment was above a bar in midtown Detroit, a gentrified neighborhood just north of downtown that had become a magnet for young idealists like Holly.

The bar was managed by Tom Flickinger. A bald, 40ish former construction worker from my old neighborhood, Tom was a politics and history junkie who loved Detroit's sports teams. He was smart and opinionated, with a cup-is-half-empty take on current events. We had a lot in common. Whenever I was in Detroit, for work or for business, I would meet Holly in the bar, where she was a regular, and pass the time chatting with Tom. I liked the guy, but there was something I didn't know about him.

He was dating my daughter.

"He's what?" I said when Lori told me about the relationship. They had been dating for months but were afraid to tell us. An authoritative parent, Lori told Holly that we'd support whatever—and whoever—she wanted in life.

Separately, Lori told me to behave. She knew I wasn't thrilled.

About a year later, Tom, Holly, Lori, and I sat around a small table in a quiet corner of a bar near our home. After dinner was ordered and the alcohol poured, Tom said, "I love Holly very much and she loves me. We're talking a lot about our future together—about getting married. I'm sure you have a lot of questions about us. We thought it would be a good idea to talk about them." Tom handled the situation perfectly, defusing our concerns with love and common sense. They married a year later.

I struggled similarly with Gabrielle's decision to drop her education major halfway through her undergraduate work at James Madison. I loved the idea of being the father of a teacher—maybe it was the notion that somehow my daughter's selfless aura would rub off on me. Instead, she wanted to be a lawyer, and I repeatedly told her the legal profession was in the midst of huge disruption. There were few decent jobs for young lawyers—and, like I had told her sister, I didn't want Gabrielle to be poor for a living.

Gabrielle wanted to use a law degree to go into

politics, specifically to work on Capitol Hill on education policy, where she thought she could help families like ours dealing with autism. "You want to go into politics?" I told Gabrielle, "Nothing gets done in this town."

She laughed. "I know. I read your columns."

I was worried enough to arrange for Gabrielle to meet several political and policy leaders in Washington, all primed with my arguments against law school. A year later, after completing an internship on Capitol Hill, Gabrielle entered law school at Michigan State University, where she's thriving.

As for Tyler, our ambitions were adjusted by the autism diagnosis. Still, I assumed he would go to a four-year college, maybe even JMU. His teachers agreed. They had seen 99 percent of their graduates matriculate in college. Tyler's grades were okay, mostly B's and C's, largely because Lori dedicated hours each week to helping Tyler where he struggled most: writing and organizing.

"You need to prepare yourself for the fact that he can't do a four-year college," Lori told me after a parent-teacher conference during Tyler's sophomore year of high school. "He may need to start at a community college."

That shouldn't have surprised me. It shouldn't have disappointed me. After all, 7.7 million students, 45 percent of all undergraduates, enrolled in public two-year colleges in the 2012–13 school year. Why did I expect more for my son? Probably for the same reason I wanted Holly to marry somebody her age and lobbied to keep Gabrielle out of law school.

Like many Americans, I tended to define success as accumulating enough money and autonomy to live comfortably. In her book *Thrive*, Arianna Huffington dismissed the traditional definition of success as money plus power, two things Huffington had accumulated in large quantities as an online publisher. "But I was not living a successful life by any sane definition of success."

What she was missing was balance—a third leg of the stool, which Huffington said consists of well-being, wisdom, wonder, and giving. It's what our grandparents called "the good life." Still in their 20s, both Holly and Gabrielle are living good lives, making their marks in all three metrics of *Thrive*. As borderline autistic, Tyler will lag behind his peers into his 20s, but his teachers and therapists agree he eventually will catch up. He will earn a living, live independently, and live happily. The good life.

Now don't get me started about grandchildren.

GELACO HERNANDEZ IS a 59-year-old native of Mexico who snuck into the United States 40 years ago, where he lived and worked in the shadows of the U.S. immigration system until a benevolent employer helped him secure citizenship. Then he moved from California to Arkansas and opened a Mexican store. He poured the profits into a Mexican restaurant, which did well enough for him to open a second restaurant. He's married with three kids, ages 11 to 18.

"It's the American dream, sir." Hernandez punctuated almost every sentence with a "sir," despite the fact that he is nearly a decade older than me and we were discussing his parental ambitions in a most informal setting: a minor league baseball park in North Little Rock. From a row of seats behind home plate, Hernandez positioned himself between me and his family—his wife, two daughters, and son—and whispered in my ear.

"I tell my kids, 'When I come to this country I didn't have no money, no father, no friends. I didn't have no house. I didn't have no papers; I was illegal. I didn't have no job. I didn't speak English. I was nothing.'" He paused to offer me a bag of unshelled peanuts, nodding toward his kids. "I consider myself a successful parent, a successful guy, because I worked all my life and saved money. But I won't be a true success until they do better than me."

That starts with a college education, Hernandez said, but his 18-year-old son doesn't want to go. He wants to work in his father's restaurants. "He's not too good. He's a lazy one," Hernandez sniffed. "He's a momma's boy, so he gets away with a lot." At home before the game, Hernandez and his son had had another fight over the boy's future.

The father yelled, "I'm worried about you! You don't want to be like me."

"You're not doing so badly," the son replied. "You're selling tacos. That's not so bad."

"You can do better," Hernandez snapped. "You must do better. You need to go to college, marry a college girl, and become a professional."

If the Hernandez family is at all typical, the son will be a success—if not precisely on his father's terms. A study of more than 5,000 immigrants' children led by sociologist Rubén G. Rumbaut found that an overwhelming number of them felt "motivated to achieve" because of a gnawing need to redeem their parents' sacrifices. The younger Hernandez likely will feel that tug.

Several related studies suggest that Asian immigrant parents impose pressure on their kids to uphold the "family honor." In short, parental pressure is more overt among immigrant parents than among parents who are white and deeply rooted in this country. "White American parents have been found to be more focused on building children's social skills and self-esteem," wrote Yale Law School professors Amy Chua and Jed Rubenfeld in a *New York Times* preview of their book, *The Triple Package*, about the rise and fall of cultural groups in America.

They say there's an ocean of difference between "You're amazing, Mommy and Daddy never want you to worry about a thing," and "If you don't do well at school, you'll let down the family and end up a bum on the streets." Neither approach is ideal. In a study of thousands of high school students, the authors noted, Asian American students reported the lowest self-esteem of any racial group, even as they posted the highest grades.

Which brings me back to Megan Chung. She's the 16-year-old prodigy I introduced you to in Chapter 2—the girl who told a group of Arkansas seventh-graders that her mother pushed her to excel. She smiled and giggled, calling her mother "my tiger mom." After her speech, I introduced myself to Megan and told her I was writing about parental expectations.

"Oh," she replied with a grin, "you could write a chapter on my mom. She's always saying, 'I want you to go to Harvard.' All Korean moms want their kids to go to Harvard so they can say, 'My daughter goes to Harvard.' Not that I want to go to Harvard. It's more for her than for me." Assuming that Megan was exaggerating, I asked if I could meet her mother. Megan said yes, and we arranged to grab coffee the next day.

I was sitting in a coffee shop two blocks from the Bill Clinton Presidential Library when Megan walked in with her mother. Laurie Chung looked not much older than her daughter. She was wearing a tailored pantsuit and carried herself with the confident bearing of some-body successful in business. Mrs. Chung, a native of South Korea, told me that she owned two businesses—and yes, she expected Megan to attend Harvard.

"I have four kids," she said. "I want them all to grow up and be successful so they will have a stable job, a good income, and some free time. I want them to be professionals," she said. "You know, doctors and lawyers, like that."

But why Harvard? "I want her to go to a top university. She has such great potential," the mom said. "But I wouldn't make her go if she doesn't like it."

Megan rolled her eyes and laughed. "I know this about Mom," she said, gently rubbing her mother's arm. "She can't wait to tell her friends, 'Oh, my daughter goes to Harvard. I'm such a great parent.'"

Mrs. Chung nodded. If Megan gets into Harvard, she said, "I'm going to Harvard, too."

Megan balled her fists. "If I make a mistake, it's not my mom's fault. If I do well, it's not her success. When I gave a speech recently, all kinds of people complimented me. She didn't even come to the speech." For a moment Megan spoke to me as if her mother wasn't at the same table.

Mrs. Chung said flatly, "I didn't know about the speech."

"Why?" Megan said. "I told you about it." Then she looked away from her mother and at me. "These are my accomplishments, the grades and the piano.

They're not hers," Megan said. "I know my mom pays for the lessons, but I'm the one who does the practices."

I was struck by the lack of anger in Megan's tone and the lack of apology in her mother's. Judging by their clinical approach to the conversation, this wasn't their first conflict. Megan acknowledged that pressure has many sources. About half comes from within: "I'm wired competitively and would be type A, I think, under any circumstances." Another quarter, she said, comes from teachers, peers, coaches, and other social pressures. Her mother accounts for the final quarter.

I asked Megan what she's learned from her mother that she'll carry into adulthood. Specifically, does she think it's better to raise kids with too few expectations or too many? "Too few," she quickly answered. "You might have the most brilliant, perfect child in the world, but if you overwhelm them with expectations, they'll break."

Mrs. Chung shook her head and smiled. "You're not going to break, Megan." She sipped her coffee. "And you're going to Harvard to be a professional."

I'm getting awfully tired of reading how my father bought me the election. I think of all the things I did—I was the one out there.

JOHN F. KENNEDY, 1961

6

HAPPY

"Dream Big, but Don't Expect Too Much"

Charlottesville, Virginia—*From 30 yards or 30 inches, the façade of Thomas Jefferson's mansion, Monticello, appears to be constructed of sturdy beige bricks. On closer examination, it becomes clear that Jefferson actually built his home of sand-blown wood. Running his hand along a front wall, Tyler says, "Phony."*

We're here for me to think through the question of what makes a happy child. What better place to begin than the home of the man who enshrined "pursuit of happiness" in the Declaration of Independence? "We can't leave here until you tell me what makes you happy, Tyler."

He slaps me with a tour brochure and jokes, "That's what makes me happy."

The 33-room mansion sits atop a dark, narrow tunnel through which slaves would lug platters of food, ice, beer, wine, and tableware for Jefferson and his two or three dozen guests dining just above the secret channel. When the wine ran out, Jefferson would open a panel in the side of the fireplace, insert the empty bottle, and then reach into a hidden dumbwaiter, where a slave had secreted a full bottle for Jefferson to grab with a flourish. Astonished guests also saw plates of hot food mysteriously appear on a revolving door fitted with shelves. Long after dinner, the slaves would walk to their cabins along Mulberry Row, a living hell so well hidden that visitors didn't know of its existence, just a stone's throw from their dining table.

In designing the mansion, Henry Wiencek wrote in Smithsonian *magazine, Jefferson followed a principle conceived two centuries earlier by Palladio: "We must contrive a building in such a manner that the finest and most noble parts of it be the most exposed to public view, and the less agreeable disposed in by places, and removed from sight as much as possible."*

I'm overwhelmed by the thought of Monticello as a metaphor for parenthood. It is human nature for mothers and fathers to expose only the finest and most noble features of their children to public view—to remove from sight the less agreeable features. But we go further. We create and perpetuate myths about our children: They're brilliant and gorgeous and popular and successful and damn near perfect, a reflection of their moms and dads. These stories are as deceptive as sand-blown wood and hidden dumbwaiters. Like historians' portrayals of Jefferson as a "benevolent slaveholder," parents' images of their children can be gauzy contradictions in the service of lies.

In this house of paradox called Monticello lived the

founding father who wrote "all men are created equal" in the Declaration of Independence, and whose first draft excoriated the slave trade as an "assemblage of horrors," a "cruel war against human nature itself." And yet, somewhere in the late 1780s and 1790s, Jefferson embraced the economics of slavery—actually calculating in a letter to George Washington that he was making a 4 percent profit every year on the birth of black children. He ordered slaves whipped and sold farther south. Historians believe Jefferson was the father of the six children of Sally Hemings, a slave at Monticello.

For the last few minutes of our tour, Tyler and I trace the steps of those slaves—in the tunnel below the mansion, along Mulberry Row, and on the wide lawn behind the back porch, where shortly after Jefferson's death entire families were broken apart and sold like cattle. "I'm beginning to learn," my boy says, "that things are never as they seem."

Aspies aren't big on metaphors. They tend to be literal and pragmatic; Tyler certainly is wired that way. Which is why I consider the brief conversation we had in the car driving away from Monticello to be a breakthrough.

"I'll make you a deal, Tyler. You don't have to do your homework in the car if you will talk to me about this amazing paradox. I mean, one of the founding fathers of freedom was a slaveholder. And your father—I wanted you to be happy, but on my terms. What's with that?"

Tyler chuckles at the lame founding father/Fournier father comparison. "Okay, I'll pursue your happiness." He tosses his textbooks in the backseat and turns serious: "You love writing. I can barely pick up a pencil. You love playing sports, and I was never a sports guy."

"Yes." I say, "What do you make of that?"

"Kids aren't always going to be like you," he says. "My kids could grow up to be freaking jocks, for all I know."

I'm stunned. I can't believe he's opening up, even this little. It's rare to hear him talk about his future, let alone fatherhood. I balance my notebook on the steering wheel and start scribbling at 60 mph. "I'd approve of them playing sports," Tyler tells me, and laughs. "Heck, I'd even go to their games!"

I protest: He won't go to sporting events with me. "Yes, but you're my dad, not my kids. I'll do what my kids need me to do."

I ask whether he felt pushed into sports.

"I guess, but you never said, 'You've got to play baseball, Tyler.' You said, "Hey, buddy, want to play ball?' I knew you wanted me to play. I knew it was important to you that we play together. So I did. I did it for you."

I circle back to the happiness paradox—how I wanted him to be happy, but my actions might have had the opposite effect. "Were you happy as a little kid?" I wince, afraid of the answer.

"I'd say so."

Now?

"Am I happy now? I'd say so. My kind of happy."

"*But you don't have many friends.*"

"*That's the problem,*" Tyler objects. *His tone is matter-of-fact, not accusatory or defensive.* "*You have a picture in your head of what makes a kid happy. But then you have a kid and it doesn't turn out that way. That just means your picture didn't come true. It doesn't mean I'm not happy. I have a different picture.*"

"*Are you happy in your picture?*"

"*Most of the time, yes,*" he says. "*Are you always happy in yours?*"

"*No, buddy. Not always.*"

"*Same with me.*"

MY CHILDHOOD IS a buffet of happy memories, including one that evokes a shivery blast of Canadian air, acres of smooth ice, and the bittersweet aroma of hot chocolate on sweaty gloves. We were playing hockey on a frozen Lake Erie—me and my two brothers, Mike and Tim, and our best pals, three Canadian brothers who lived near our parents' cottage outside Windsor, Ontario. A half mile from shore, the only sounds on the lake were ours. "I'm open!" "Nice shot!" Laughter, so much laughter, and background noise: the clatter of wooden sticks and steel blades at work, grinding delicate lines into the hard surface.

I was maybe 10 years old. The other boys were younger, but not much. My dad was there, too, towering over us at nearly seven feet tall in skates. His shadow was as long as the makeshift rink as he glided around us during a game of keep-away—him vs. us. We could have been pylons for what little chance we had to steal the puck, which seemed tethered tightly to Dad's stick by an invisible string. "Mr. Fournier, we give up!" one of the boys shouted. They worshipped Dad. My brothers and I did, too. He was the dad who played with the neighborhood kids all day and partied with their parents all night. The neighbor who showed up when something needed to be fixed, built, or solved. The big guy. The funny guy. The good guy. The Guy: That's what Dad tried to be.

"I give up, too," he called with a grin, passing the puck softly across the ice to the kid who'd called it quits. "Good game. You guys take it from here. Let me see if I can find you better ice." Dad sat in a snow-drift and changed into boots, then walked away from our game, away from shore. He kicked away snow in search of a smoother patch of ice for 50 yards . . . 100 yards . . . 150 yards, and suddenly . . . *splash!* I looked up from the game in time to see Dad pulling himself out of the lake. Dripping wet and sprawled across the ice on his stomach, Dad spun himself around and dipped a hand into the hole to fish his boots out of 15 feet of water.

He could have died, but that thought never crossed my mind. Dad was invulnerable, I thought, unstoppable. Shivering and clutching the boots to his chest, he lumbered back to the hockey game and warned us about the thin ice. "Skate around the hole," he winked. His wet clothes stiffened in the frosty air as Dad walked the half mile to the cottage. "The ice is fine," he told Mom as we piled though the door. "It's the water that's a bitch." Mom wrapped Dad in a blanket and poured him a glass of Crown Royal. "No ice," he said, melting Mom's look of stern disapproval. We boys giggled.

Four decades later, that memory came to mind while I was reading a book called *The Childhood Roots of Adult Happiness* by Dr. Edward M. Hallowell, a clinical psychiatrist and a father of three. In its first pages, the doctor recalled a happy childhood memory: tobogganing near his Massachusetts home after a massive snowstorm. "I didn't know it at the time, but I was . . . doing what I recommend in this book," Hallowell wrote. "I was learning how to create and sustain joy, a tremendously important skill. I was also acquiring the all-important qualities of playfulness, optimism, a can-do attitude, and connectedness—qualities that have deepened in me since then, qualities that make me, for the most part, a happy man."

Can you remember a happy day from your own childhood? Chances are it channels the attributes that Hallowell called the keys to raising happy children: optimism, playfulness, self-esteem ("can-do attitude"), and the sense of being a part of something greater than yourself ("connectedness"). Consider my memory.

Optimism: I *knew* Dad would be okay when he fell through the ice.

Playfulness: Hockey on a shoveled piece of lake, boots for goalposts, and snowbanks for sideboards.

Self-esteem: No trophies for the losers. Actually, no trophies for anybody. But everything about that game (and sports, in general) made me feel better about myself. Practice didn't make me perfect, but it made me better. I couldn't win them all, but I could do my best. I hated to lose, but I learned to grow from defeat.

Connectedness: These were my brothers, my friends, and my dad—and we came together one wintry day and created the very thing every parent says they want for their kids: happiness.

I asked once on Twitter, "Parents, you say you want your kids to grow up 'happy.' What does that mean?'" The answers were as wise as anything you'll find in the typical be-a-better-parent book. "I tell my kids it's not my job to make them happy," wrote Beth Anne Mumford. "Love them with all my being, but happy is not the same as 'good person.'"

"Happy is the wrong goal," added Andrew Siegel, father of twin boys. "The goal should be to want your kids to be good people." Tom Anderson said, "Having the tools to boldly take life by the horns and pursue their calling."

Don Graber tweeted his meaning of childhood happiness: "Godly, appreciative, humble, confident, capable, big dreams & real expectations, wise, discerning, kind [and] compassionate." I asked him via email to explain what he meant by "real expectations." He replied, "It sounds a bit contradictory: Dream big, but don't expect too much. But that's not all." He wrote:

> I have two daughters. My oldest is eight and the younger will be four next month. The younger is still in the "tag-along" stage. Mimicking her sister and basically being as big of a ham as possible to get as much attention as possible. Not many independent interests as of yet. The older however is very involved in Irish step dancing. She is in a performance company as well as participating in competitions. Essentially this is her life outside school. She loves it, she is good at it, and if you ask her what she wants to be when she grows up she will tell you without hesitation that she wants to be an Irish dance teacher and have her own school. Her interest in competitions is growing as well, and wants to eventually go to Worlds.
>
> My wife and I are obviously very supportive of this and do everything we can to help her. How-

ever, we do not hold her hand or coddle her. If she is going to be serious about dancing and competing she needs to have the confidence and discipline to achieve it. Real confidence does not come from people telling you how great and wonderful you are. It comes from work. It comes from achieving something. She cannot be shielded from criticism and failure. She needs to experience that in order to grow and improve, in order to have the capability to do those things. She needs to know that she will not always win, she will make mistakes, she needs to work her butt off, and in turn she will appreciate her victories when they come.

So, I love that she has these dreams of winning Worlds, becoming a dance teacher, and starting her own school. I love that, and I want to do everything I can to help her. And that includes keeping her grounded in reality. She won't always win, but that doesn't mean she shouldn't try. I want her to do what she loves, but she can't have so much of her identity wrapped up in it that failure would destroy her. She needs drive and passion, but also a healthy sense of self.

I can almost guarantee that Graber's girls are growing up happy. He and his wife are defying the conventional wisdom of modern parenting, which has led parents to believe that exposing kids to negative emotions will hurt them. Most children are shielded against injury, embarrassment, and the many other flavors of failure that can actually make them stronger. Bubble-wrapped kids never learn how to deal effectively with their emotions.

In his book *Positive Pushing*, Jim Taylor calls "emotional mastery" the first of three keys to a child's success. The second is self-esteem. The third is a sense of ownership of their course in life. When a parent takes charge of a child's academic success and interests outside school, the kid loses ownership—the sense that life's ups and downs are in the kid's own hands, not Mom's and Dad's. The goal is to help your child do the hard things "because I want to," rather than "because I've got to."

Hallowell put it this way: "Life is a game of multiple failures. The people who prevail in life—who become happy in themselves as adults—are the ones who can fail or suffer loss or defeat but never lose heart."

What other paths to happiness can we find in Graber's note? There's optimism: "She has these dreams of winning." Martin Seligman, a pioneer of research on happiness, found that optimism protects against depression and anxiety later in life. While genetics play a role in a person's optimism, Seligman determined the attribute can be learned at an early age.

Graber's older girl also is playing, which we know is an important part of a child's development: "She loves it, she is good at it." Drawing from the research of psychology professor Mihaly Csikszentmihalyi, Hallowell concluded, "Play generates joy. Play becomes its own reward." It's a key to happiness.

Finally, Graber's older daughter is experiencing what researchers call "connectedness," forming bonds with her parents, her dance troupe, her sister, and even her Irish roots. Hallowell said nature gives *almost* all children and parents the ability to connect. He wrote: "I say 'almost' because some children are born with problems in making meaningful connections with others: These are the children with autism, Asperger's syndrome, childhood schizophrenia, or pervasive developmental disorder."

I wrote in the margins of his book, a few days after touring Monticello, *Can Tyler connect? Yes!*

THE TRIP TO Jefferson's home was not in pursuit of happiness. It was in pursuit of understanding. Tyler is fundamentally optimistic and playful, blessed with a unique spirit that I can only call self-esteem. His autism and my obtuseness hid those attributes from me for years.

I thought an optimistic boy must be swaggering, popular, and ambitious. In Tyler, optimism is a steely, quiet confidence: *"My kind of happy."*

I thought playfulness was best exhibited through sports, like a pack of boys lacing up skates on a frozen lake. For Tyler, video games (in moderation) are a healthy outlet, and I'm starting to think there's something special about his dry sense of humor: *I'll pursue your happiness.*

I thought fathers and sons could only connect through sports—and then one day I'm wiping away tears at the home of a dead president: *I knew it was important for you that we play together. So I did. I did it for you.*

MY CONVERSATIONS WITH parents almost always start with a basic question: "What expectations do you have for your children as they grow up?" The answer almost always begins with some variation of "All I want is for them to be happy." But I wonder, is that really *all* they want? After all, I'm sure there are happy serial killers. Think of all the happy assholes you know. "Why is it that bad people can be happy?" wrote Marc Gellman in a 2006 essay for *Newsweek* magazine. "The reason is that happiness as defined by our culture has become just a synonym for pleasure, and anyone can feel pleasure."

I highly recommend Gellman's essay, "An Argument Against Happiness," because it blows conventional wisdom to smithereens. The synonym for *happiness* is not *pleasure*, he wrote. It's *goodness*. "True happiness, the kind of happiness we ought to wish for our children and for ourselves is almost always the result of doing hard but good things over and over."

People tell researchers that getting married didn't make them any happier, and neither did having children or making a lot of money. That's because happiness for most people is defined as pleasure, and most of what makes a marriage or parenthood fulfilling is not very pleasurable. But it is good.

The unbounded pursuit of pleasure is harmful. Researchers in the booming field of positive psychology see a direct link between increasing cultural emphasis on materialism and status and the rising rates of depression, paranoia, and psychopathology. People who focus on living with a sense of purpose are more likely to remain healthy and intellectually sound and even to live longer than people who focus on achieving feelings of "happiness" via pleasure.

There is nothing wrong with the pleasure that comes with a big meal, a sexy night, or victory on the playing field—but it's fleeting. Raising kids, working through marriage troubles, and volunteering at a soup kitchen may be less pleasurable, but these pursuits provide fulfillment—a sense that you're the best person you can be. Researchers call this "hedonic well-being" and link it directly to lower levels of cardiovascular disease, Alzheimer's disease, and other maladies. The research appears consistent at every income and education level, and among all races.

This reminds me of a family story. When my brothers were in their teens, they delivered televisions for an appliance store in suburban Detroit. One day they were assigned a delivery in an achingly poor and crime-ridden Detroit neighborhood. After installing the TV, my brothers were walking out of the apartment building when they noticed a familiar form headed toward them, a huge man wearing jeans and a T-shirt. It was Dad's day off, and he looked startled at first—then a bit angry.

"What are you boys doing down here?" Dad said, sternly. "This is a bad neighborhood." He was carrying two bags of our clothes—pants and shirts that we had outgrown.

Tim asked, "What are *you* doing down here?"

Dad shrugged. "Just seeing some people I know."

At this point in our lives, we already knew Dad couldn't pass a stranded driver; he always stopped to help. I once saw him shake hands with a homeless man outside a Red Wings game, discreetly passing a couple of crumpled dollar bills to the guy he called Bill. "Thank you, Ron," the man said.

What do I ultimately want for my kids? I want them to pursue the happiness that is found in goodness. On a day off, I want them to bring outgrown clothes to a bad neighborhood.

You know about one of the happiest days of my childhood, playing pickup hockey on Lake Erie. Now

I'll tell you about one of the happiest days of my *adult* life: June 29, 2013, the day my eldest daughter, Holly, married Tom Flickinger at St. Patrick's Catholic Church near their home in Detroit. Lori and I arrived from Washington a few days before the wedding and focused on getting our parents to the ceremony.

Lori's mother was rapidly fading from dementia, which was making her antisocial and combative, unwilling even to be diagnosed or treated. Her decline was devastating to watch, as Shirley Rumpz had been a loving wife, mother, and grandmother—a sharp, dynamic woman who ran her household and the University of Detroit union negotiations with no-nonsense efficiency. Now she was talking about skipping her granddaughter's wedding.

As for my father, four years had passed since I first noticed his decline. For his 70th birthday, my brothers, my sister, Raquel, and I arranged to have Dad throw out the first pitch at a minor league baseball game in Grand Rapids. It seemed a perfect gift. He loved baseball and still looked game-ready. Mom tried to talk us out of it, saying Dad would be embarrassed by the attention. "Nonsense," I said. "He'll love it." But when Dad arrived at the park and learned of our plans, he got angry and refused to take the field. I threw the pitch for him.

"What's up with Dad?" I asked Mom.

She said, "Everything's fine, honey."

Everything wasn't fine. In addition to the "mild neuropathy" that our parents had told us about and minimized, a neurologist had diagnosed Dad with Parkinson's disease. Dad dismissed the diagnosis, and Mom enabled his denial. He was The Guy, a prideful man whose self-image was built on the myth of his invulnerability, and inflated by every person who idolized him—his friends, his co-workers, his neighbors, and, most important to him, his four kids and wife. Mom covered for Dad out of respect for his pride. She loved this strong man her entire life, and wouldn't let go easily.

In the decades-old mythology of our family, Ronald and Florence Fournier were the perfect couple, and the stubborn refusal to forsake that myth kept Dad from acknowledging and treating his disease. Expectations were, literally, killing him. A few months before Holly's wedding, my brother Tim and I confronted our father. Sitting on Tim's backyard patio in Grand Rapids, sipping a light beer, Dad said he'd accept the diagnosis and begin treatment (albeit five years or so after the initial diagnosis) on one condition: He didn't want us steamrolling Mom, intruding on her control of their lives and his treatment. "Respect your mother."

When our parents arrived for the wedding, Lori had them sit in the back of the church so they wouldn't have far to walk in the procession. Dad slowly, painfully, eased himself into the wooden pew and flashed me a weak smile. He looked small, hunched, and spent. I crouched close to his ear and whispered, "Thanks for coming, Dad." Then, without thinking, I kissed him on the cheek. I hadn't kissed my father in 45 years. I was surprised how natural it felt—the softness of his skin and the smell of his body so close.

"I wouldn't have missed it for the world," he said. The reporter in me knew better. My parents damn near missed the wedding, in part because they didn't want family and friends to see him so frail.

When it came time to form the procession line, Dad told me, "I got to take a piss."

"Can't it wait?"

"No," he said. The bathroom was at the front of the church, near the altar, so Dad had to walk past family and friends awaiting the ceremony's start. Some checked their watches, while others whispered or nodded in sympathy as Dad baby-stepped from the back of the church to the front, a trip I could make in less than a minute. It took Dad ten times as long. For such a proud man, this was hell, and I don't know whether I've ever been so impressed.

Mom was angry. She had wanted to stay home to protect Dad's dignity and health, and came only after intense lobbying by me and Tim. I was a mix of emotions: proud of Dad's effort up the aisle, but angry at his sickness—and at my parents for not seeking treatment for him sooner.

Finally, my father and Lori's mother joined their spouses in the procession line, and the wedding began. I now was able to focus on Holly and walk her down the aisle. Halfway to the altar, I asked her how she was doing. "Fine," Holly said with a smile, squeezing my arm. She never took her focus off Tom as we approached the altar. I lifted Holly's veil, kissed my daughter, and told her I loved her. Then I shook Tom's hand, noticing for the first time that tears were streaming down his face. My doubts evaporated. *Man, he does love her.*

After the service, I walked out with my parents, trying to convince them to attend the reception. Mom insisted Dad wasn't up to it, and said they were going to the hotel. I buckled his seat belt and was closing the door when I heard Lori calling for us. It was time for a family photo, she said, and Holly wanted my parents in it. I asked Mom if Dad could handle the short walk across the street. She pursed her lips and said, "You have to ask your father." I leaned into the car to speak to Dad, but Mom interrupted. She sounded desperate, almost pleading: "His pants. His zipper." Dad's fly was down. He could no longer zip himself up.

MY PARENTS DIDN'T make the reception. Lori's parents managed to attend for a bit, although her mother, Shirley, seemed confused and agitated. In a quiet tribute to her grandmother, whom the kids called Nanny, Holly wrapped around her bouquet a locket that once belonged to Shirley's own grandmother. "I knew past-Nanny would have been so touched," Holly said.

The next morning, I swallowed my disappointment and visited my parents in their hotel room. They looked exhausted. The brief wedding ceremony had drained Dad. Worry had worn Mom. I gave them the highlights of the reception and leaned closer to Dad as he whispered, "I can't believe you're taking this so well."

"What?" I replied.

"I messed up the wedding."

I wasn't sure if he was referring to delaying the ceremony, missing the reception, or something else. Was he ashamed of how sick and old he looked? No, he couldn't be that vain—not the guy who'd taught me to be good, do my best, and not worry about what other people think.

"You mean, the trouble you had walking down the aisle?"

"Yes."

"Hell, Dad, you did great. You did what Holly needed you to do. Despite what's going on now." I couldn't say it—*Parkinson's.*

"Thank you, Rock," Dad said, calling me by the nickname he had given me before I was born. (He had been a fan of the baseball star Rocky Colavito.) "That means the world to me. I can't tell you what that means. I hope I didn't let you down."

My stomach clenched. Dad's words reminded me of his grandson and of the evening at the White House when Tyler had awaited his turn to meet the Obamas. *I hope I don't let you down, Dad.*

The wedding was a hard and happy event. Notice that this story doesn't include memories of big feasts, boozy laughter, and illicit romance—though, for the record, the reception at the Detroit Historical Museum (and the post-reception party at Tom's bar) included such pleasures.

What sticks with me are the small acts of goodness: My father and mother-in-law swallowed their pride and came; my mother let down her defenses; my son-in-law cried at the sight of his new bride; my daughter paid quiet tribute to "past-Nanny"; and Lori insisted we take a family photo for Holly. It would be the last photo with all of us together.

It almost didn't happen. *His pants. His zipper.* I'll never forget how Dad looked down at his crotch and then at me. "It's okay," I said, zipping his fly closed. That's when I convinced him to get out of the car and pose for the photo. I could see the pain and shame in his face. He could see Holly and Lori waiting. He was still The Guy, full of goodness.

All I had to say was, "It'll make the girls happy, Dad."

I believe . . . that every human mind feels pleasure in doing good to another.

THOMAS JEFFERSON, IN A LETTER TO
JOHN ADAMS, OCTOBER 14, 1816

Part Two

WHAT
WE NEED

7

GRIT

"He Talked a Lot About Himself and His Stuff"

Little Rock, Arkansas—*The road trips are coming to an end. Lori had wanted me to bond with Tyler, to understand him better, and to grow closer to him. She wanted Tyler to interact with a world mostly unlike him—with "neurologically typical" people, who instinctively socialize, empathize, and read social clues.*

Our first stop was the White House, where I felt the shame I had caused Tyler. Then we toured the homes and libraries of Theodore Roosevelt, John and John Quincy Adams, Gerald Ford, John Kennedy, and Thomas Jefferson, where I began to rightsize my dreams and realize I needed to help Tyler develop his. Each of these trips forced me to think more broadly—beyond just Tyler and even his sisters—and wonder: Why do we do this to our kids?

I read child development books and studies, interviewed experts, and met dozens of parents in search of answers. And then former presidents George W. Bush and Bill Clinton agreed to meet privately with Tyler. He's going to visit Clinton today at his library in Little Rock, and eight days later, Bush at his Dallas office.

I'm not sure why they agreed to do this. While I respect both men, I never spared my criticism during their presidencies, and now, retired from elected office, neither Clinton nor Bush would expect their favors returned. I chalk it up to something you don't hear much about in politics: decency. Like most politicians, the former presidents are public servants at their core. Far from perfect (as journalists like me never fail to point out), most men and women who enter politics are fundamentally good people in a bad system. But that's another book.

A therapist once called Tyler courageous, which I simply hadn't understood. How could a boy afraid of bees, needles, and dark rooms be brave? But this young man who faces up to his fear—to introduce himself to new people every day, for instance—might be the bravest person I know. The therapist had said Tyler was more determined to learn how to make social connections than anybody else in his practice. "It would be very easy for him to just give up, but he keeps coming back and tries to make those connections."

We're standing at the back of a news conference at the Clinton library. The governor-turned-president is talking to reporters about education policy, just moments before our scheduled meeting. Tyler tugs at my elbow. His face is pale. "I don't want to do this," he says. "You interview him, please."

I tell him no—and not to worry: "You'll do fine, buddy." But the truth is, I'm not so sure.

"LET ME SHOW you around, Tyler," Bill Clinton said
as he opened the door to the suite atop his presidential
library, a 68,698-square-foot fortress jutting over the
Arkansas River like a half-finished bridge. His pent-
house is long and narrow, like the shotgun shacks that
once dotted rural Arkansas, but much longer, wider,
and brighter, with polished blond wood floors and an
art collection befitting a head of state. An imposing
west-facing wall flanked the bedroom, an oval-shaped
office, a dining room, and a den with floor-to-ceiling
windows that gave Clinton a full view of Little Rock:
the city that launched both of our careers—his as a
politician and mine, far less auspiciously, as a reporter.

Standing at the windows, Clinton and I pointed to
downtown buildings and lost ourselves in the 1980s:
the Capitol Dome, beneath which we both worked;
the shuttered remains of a storied newspaper; the headquarters of one of Clinton's first political benefactors. I
pointed to a hotel dominating the skyline and said, "I
remember interviewing you there about rumors that
you were running for president." (What I didn't say: A
state employee named Paula Jones later accused Clinton of sexually harassing her in that hotel just moments
before my interview with him.)

"I don't remember that," Clinton replied. "I do remember those days, though, Ron. We've come a ways."

I reminded Clinton of the time, early in his

presidency, when he took an emotional tour of war-
ring neighborhoods in Northern Ireland before stopping in a market that had been bombed just 18 months
prior. "You turned around from a fruit stand, saw me
standing there taking notes, and said, 'Man, this is a
long way from Arkansas.'"

Clinton smiled. "I remember *that*."

So much to remember. Toward the end of Clin-
ton's first year in office, less than a year after moving to
Washington, Lori and I attended the traditional press
corps holiday party at the White House. In the reception line, the Clintons greeted us warmly. The First
Lady asked me about Holly and Gabrielle. She had
known the girls well enough in Arkansas to remember
their names. The president asked Lori, "How are you
guys settling in?"

Lori replied, "We miss Arkansas."

We weren't very happy in Washington. I was traveling too much, and when I was home, I often was
too tired and impatient with Lori and the kids. White-
water, health care reform, the White House travel office—a bad political year for the Clintons had made
1993 a banner year for my career, and a lousy time for
my family. My work-life balance was out of whack,
and would remain so for years.

Lori joked to Clinton, "We should all go back to
Arkansas."

The president laughed. "As if."

Three years later, Clinton and Lori would have

a laugh on me. A cell phone malfunction allowed Lori to overhear me teasing a female colleague about "sleeping" with another reporter, a seatmate aboard Air Force One. A sexist double entendre. Fortunately, Lori knew I wasn't serious and told me to knock it off. Unfortunately, the gaffe got to Clinton, who decided to make me squirm. This is where it gets bizarre. The president of the United States called my wife from the plane. "Hello, Lori? This is Bill Clinton."

Lori thought it was a joke—and an imposter. "Well, hello, Mr. President," she deadpanned. "I need to make this quick. Cher is at the door."

Clinton plowed ahead. "I just wanted to let you know that when we left Little Rock last night, Ron wasn't with us. He might have taken up with some ladies." That's right: As a practical joke, Bill Clinton insinuated that *I* was unfaithful.

"Oh, that's okay, Mr. President," Lori said. "He loves Little Rock."

Later that day, Clinton asked me what Lori thought about the call. "She didn't believe it was you," I said.

Clinton laughed so hard his face turned red. "Oh," he said. "That explains a lot!"

TYLER WAS BORED. While Clinton and I stared out the window at downtown Little Rock, lost in our memories, Tyler pointed to a picture on a shelf. "It's hard to find a picture of two polar bears fighting," he said.

"You like that?" Clinton enthused. "You interested in polar bears?"

"Yes," Tyler replied. Then he repeated himself, as he tended to do, at warp speed. "It'shardtofindapicture oftwopolarbearsfighting."

"Take it." Clinton pulled the picture off the shelf, and I realized that it was actually the cover of a book called *Polar Dance: Born of the North Wind*.

"No, sir," Tyler said, "I couldn't possibly accept this."

Clinton insisted, "It's yours," and Tyler hugged the book to his chest.

It was a gracious thing for Clinton to do. Inscribed with a bookplate—"President William Jefferson Clinton. Hillary Rodham Clinton"—the volume had obviously meant enough to the former president to be displayed in his private suite.

I was equally impressed with Tyler, who until a few months prior to the visit would not have known how to handle such a delicate social interaction. He had just learned to greet Lori after school: "And how was your day?" Lori would answer with the details of her day and ask Tyler about his. "Good," he'd reply before repeating, "And how was your day?" What comes naturally to most people is a practiced and circular loop for Tyler. Caring about our day doesn't come naturally to Aspies, because they're wired to view their world inward rather than outward.

Clinton showed us to a sunlit corner of the pent-house with a small table and three overstuffed chairs. From my seat, removed a bit from their knee-to-knee conversation, I slowly watched my son transform. He sat rigid at first, his white-knuckled hands gripping the chair's brown leather arms.

"I'm a *huuuge* Theodore Roosevelt fan," Clinton said, stretching out his vowel. "I read in the notes my staff gave me for this that you were a big Roosevelt fan, and the moment in history when he was president . . . was the moment in history that most closely approximates the period I served, in the sense that we were moving from a rural to urban economy under Teddy . . ."

And off he went. If you covered Clinton, worked for Clinton, or spent any time around Clinton, you've heard this riff: Roosevelt was the bridge to the 20th century, just as the Clinton presidency was the bridge to the 21st. Income inequality . . . new technology . . . land conservation . . . and peace.

"I had to figure out things like how to spread information technology through every aspect of the economy faster, how to make it more accessible to people who didn't have money, how to make sure it was in all the schools so kids could learn about it as quickly as possible; because then there weren't nearly as many personal computers as people have in homes as now," Clinton said.

He was in professor mode—a brilliant and verbose personality who, as an extraordinarily accessible governor, earned an irreverent nickname from some members of the Little Rock press corps: "Monologue Man."

Clinton continued: "We didn't even have email when I first became president. Email was all interoffice except for a few research projects. When I became president, the average cell phone weighed 5 pounds and there were 50 sites on the World Wide Web and when I left there were like 50 million and so I was into all that. And also when Roosevelt became president we were becoming a world power, you know, he fought at San Juan Hill against the Spanish occupation of Cuba . . ."

GRIT IS IT. If there was one attribute I could teach to my children, particularly one like Tyler with a label that isolates him, it would be what psychology professor Angela Duckworth described as "perseverance and passion for long-term goals." Based on research into the lives of famous historical leaders, Duckworth and her co-authors in 2007 created a "grit scale" to determine how well people overcome adversity while maintaining motivation and enthusiasm.

George Washington, Abe Lincoln, and Franklin Roosevelt must have been off the charts—leaders who plowed past great suffering en route to greatness. When he declared, "The only thing we have to fear is fear itself," Roosevelt was appealing to the populace's true grit.

Bill Clinton never knew his biological father. His stepfather was an abusive drunk. His political career seemed over in 1980, when Arkansas voters tossed him from the governor's office after one term. His presidency nearly collapsed in 1998, over the Monica Lewinsky affair. Historians will long debate his place in history, but nobody can say Clinton lacked persistence.

There are other words for it. *Courageous* is what I wrote in my datebook the night Tyler looked into Obama's eyes, shook his hand, and said, "It's a pleasure to meet you, Mr. President." Years later, as Tyler shook hands with Clinton, I scratched another word in my notebook: *Gutty.*

With every conversation, an Aspie risks failure. It takes a special mettle, as Alan Dworkin said of his adult Aspie son, Mitch, during a telephone interview: "That guy suffered so much and yet he has been independent. He takes care of himself." I heard pain in the father's raspy voice. "He lived a horrible existence. Anytime he'd be knocked down he'd get back up again."

In his bestselling memoir, *Look Me in the Eye*, John Elder Robison, also an Aspie, wrote, "I was well into my teenage years before I figured out that I wasn't a killer, or worse. By then, I knew I wasn't being shifty or evasive when I failed to meet someone's gaze, and I had started to wonder why so many adults equated that behavior with shiftiness and evasiveness. Also, by then I had met shifty and scummy people who did look me in the eye, making me think the people who complained about me were the hypocrites."

There's not a child alive who couldn't benefit from sturdier stuff. In her 2015 essay titled "Should Schools Teach Personality?" *New York Times* staff editor Anna North described new thinking in education circles that puts a higher value on student character than on intelligence.

Her piece focused on the KIPP network of charter schools, where students learn about grit, self-control, curiosity, and four other measures of character. North quoted Leyla Bravo-Willey, the assistant principal at KIPP Infinity Middle School in Harlem. "If a child happens to be very gritty but has trouble participating in class," Willey said, "we still want them to develop that part of themselves." Of a child's character, she said, "We talk a lot about them as being skills or strengths, not necessarily traits, because it's not innate."

So there's something that Tyler has in common with his "typical" peers: Their grit is grown.

TEN MINUTES INTO the conversation with Clinton, Tyler's fingers drummed the chair and he made steady eye contact. He was accustomed to dominating conversations, and so the former president was an unfamiliar steamroller. Tyler interrupted Clinton's soliloquy on the battle of San Juan Hill: "That was the only battle worth mentioning in the Spanish-American War."

Clinton blinked four or five times, almost squinting, as he tried to simultaneously respond politely to Tyler and retake control of the conversation.

"Yeah," Clinton said. "The . . . the . . . the Spanish had colonies in the Philippines and in Cuba and Puerto Rico and we basically had a protectorate in the Philippines for a while, which was once presided over by his vice president and successor, Howard Taft. So when he fought at San Juan Hill," Clinton continued, "the idea was to not only run him out of Puerto Rico, but to run them out of Cuba, too. You know, basically keep the Americas free of colonialism."

Clinton is like Tyler in the sense that he loves to talk about what he loves to talk about. Listening to the former president ramble through thoughts on turn-of-the-century global affairs reminded me of how Aspie author David Finch referred to his own conversational style—"the verbal equivalent of a volcanic eruption, spewing mind magma in every direction." The difference is in the delivery: While Aspies tend to talk rat-a-tat fast and go off on tangents with little regard to a conversation partner, Clinton is famously deliberative and thoughtful—long pauses for emphasis as he connects disparate dots for his audiences, virtually willing them to follow his train of thought.

Shifting abruptly from the Rough Rider to the man from Hope, Clinton told Tyler: "After the Cold War when the Soviet Union collapsed and I was president, we were for a brief period the only military, economic, and political superpower in the world. And I kept telling people, 'You know, as soon as somebody gets as rich as we are, whether we are the only military superpower depends on them and not us. Because if they got the money they can spend it on whatever they want, and we better use this time to try to pull the world together.' And so that's what I tried to do."

Clinton bit his lower lip and reflected a moment, looking out the window—and not at Tyler or at me. "But I always liked Roosevelt. I liked him because he liked action and he liked reading. You know, he read a lot. He wrote more books, I think, than any president we ever had. He was very smart and he made the most of his time. And I think he was one of our 10 best presidents. He was always, I thought, wrongly . . ."

Clinton paused. "The one thing I disagreed with him on: He was also a bit too bellicose to suit me, because he was always thinking that he could never go down in history as a truly great president because he hadn't been involved in a really big war.

"He actually tried," Clinton continued on Roosevelt, "even though he died in 1919, young, he was only

61, but he'd suffered a lot. You know, he had a lot of health problems as a young child—"

"He got blind in one eye," Tyler interrupted, speaking so fast that neither Clinton nor I could quite follow.

"Yeah," Clinton said. "He tried to talk Woodrow Wilson . . . into giving him a military commission so he could fight in World War I. [He] lost one of his children in World War I."

"Quentin," Tyler said, squeezing in the name of Roosevelt's son. Clinton didn't break stride.

"And his son Ted junior, who was a brigadier general, won the Medal of Honor in World War II on D-Day," the ex-president said. "Anyway, I always liked Teddy Roosevelt and I'm glad you do. He was really a very good president."

TEDDY WAS A good father. That's my takeaway from a collection of Roosevelt's letters to his children. Edited by a Roosevelt friend shortly before the former president's death in 1919, the letters show Teddy struggling to balance his expectations against the reality of his kids' independent paths.

"This devoted father and whole-hearted companion found time to send every week a long letter of this delightful character to each of his absent children," wrote the collection's editor, Joseph Bucklin Bishop. "As the boys advanced toward manhood, the letters . . .

contain much wise suggestion and occasional admoni-
tion, the latter always administered in a loving spirit
accompanied by apology for writing in a 'preaching'
vein."

Roosevelt touches upon all the expectations boxes.
In a letter to Ted junior on October 4, 1903, the sport-
loving president tells his oldest child to keep athletics
in context. "I am delighted to have you play football. I
believe in rough, manly sports. But I do not believe in
them if they degenerate into the sole end of any one's
existence. I don't want you to sacrifice standing well
in your studies to any over-athleticism; and I need not
tell you that character counts for a great deal more than
either intellect or body in winning success in life."

Kermit received a similar letter the same month.
"I would rather have a boy of mine stand high in his
studies than high in athletics, but I could a great deal
rather have him show true manliness of character than
show either intellectual or physical prowess; and I believe you and Ted both bid fair to develop just such
character," the president wrote from the White House.

Teddy constantly reminds his kids about the importance of good grades and a solid education. And yet he
suggested to Kermit in November 1903 that average is
acceptable. "I rather suspect that you will be behind in
your studies this month," Roosevelt wrote. "If so, try
to make up next month, and keep above the middle of
the class if you can."

He had strong opinions about his boys' careers, all

delicately shared. "If you have definitely made up your mind that you have an overmastering desire to be in the Navy or the Army, and that such a career is the one in which you will take a really heartfelt interest—far more so than any other," he wrote Ted junior on January 21, 1904, "and that your greatest chance for happiness and usefulness will lie in doing this one work to which you feel yourself especially drawn—why, under such circumstances, I have but little to say."

WHEN CLINTON PAUSED to reset the conversation, I noticed Tyler's fingers again. They were carving slow, gentle circles into the chair's leather. He was comfortable with the silence. Not me. I felt that familiar tightening in my gut—worried that we were wasting Clinton's time. I wondered what he thought of Tyler, and if he was second-guessing the decision to do me this favor. I panicked. I blurted out, "What did you like about Teddy Roosevelt, Ty?"

"He had asthma and all that when he was a kid, but when he grew up he became famous for like, like, being real tough," Tyler said.

I wrote in my notebook, *Two bullied boys—TR is hope*, because that's where these two lines in my life crossed: Clinton, a man who succeeded despite a troubled youth, and Tyler, a troubled young man struggling to be a success. TR is more than their political hero. He's their role model.

"Yeah, you know, he was very frail," Clinton told Tyler.

At last, they were engaged in a real conversation, although the former president didn't seem to realize that he was repeating Tyler's points. Clinton launched again: "He had asthma as a child, and then he basically decided he would make his body strong. He became very broad and he studied boxing. And then he went out and lived in the West, lived in North Dakota, and did something that I'm particularly grateful for, because I worked hard on this when I was president: He saved the buffalo. We were down to 20 known buffalo head in the entire country and Theodore Roosevelt created the Buffalo National Park; and when I was president we lost 750 buffalo to disease in Yellowstone Park alone, and it was only half the population of Yellowstone. You know, we slowly and surely rebuilt it. And they're such a symbol of the plains, Indians, and that part of our history, it would have been tragic; and he personally saved them. If he hadn't made that park, they would have all been killed."

AFTER 45 MINUTES with one of the world's most famous men, Tyler now sat with his hands folded calmly in his lap, fingers intertwined, and knees crossed— mirroring Clinton's posture. Relaxed, confident. I thought, *He's growing before my eyes,* and now I felt guilty for all the worry, the doubts I harbored about Tyler. Damned if my stomach didn't tighten again.

Clinton's monologue had shifted from one obsession to another: coral reefs, leadership, polarization, gridlock, terrorism, national service, the joys of being a governor, the perils of new media, and the broken business models of book publishers. It was brilliant, fascinating material for a journalist like me. It was a tad boring for Tyler. Clinton didn't seem to notice or care, which struck me as odd because I knew better. I knew that Clinton is wired to connect with people—large masses of people, anyhow. But here he was: spewing mind magma . . . obsessed with certain topics . . . dominating the conversation . . . misreading a conversation partner . . .

Could it be? No, of course not, but still . . . I wrote in my notebook, *IS BC AN ASPIE????*

Suddenly I saw Tyler in another light. If the man who made empathy his calling card ("I feel your pain") can miss obvious social cues, why worry so much about my son? There is no perfect social animal—not even Bill Clinton! Maybe the autism spectrum is broader than we care to admit, and we're all on it?

I thought of something Andrew Solomon had written in *Far from the Tree*, his book about parents who struggle with their children's uniqueness. "Though many of us take pride in how different we are from our parents," Solomon wrote, "we are endlessly sad at how different our children are from us." I decided, right there in Clinton's suite, never again to regret Tyler's uniqueness.

CLINTON PULLED HIMSELF out of the chair. "I'm really glad to see you, Tyler," he said. "I have another present for you. Before I give it to you, you do not have to feel bad about it because I obtained two copies of this. It's one of my favorite books: It's the letters Theodore Roosevelt wrote to his children."

"Wow," Tyler said.

Clinton reached into a massive bookcase and pulled down a green first edition from 1919, then picked up a Sharpie, wrote inside the cover, "From another fan of Theodore Roosevelt," and signed it.

Handing it to Tyler, he repeated, "It's a very old book, but you don't have to feel bad about taking it because I have another copy, okay?" His voice was noticeably softer, reassuring—almost cooing when he hit the "okay."

"So I want you to take it and I want you to read it," Clinton continued. "You know the other thing Theodore Roosevelt did, which he would get in real trouble for today with conservatives, is he let his kids play in the White House with the animals they had. He let goats run around the White House."

Clinton laughed. Small talk wasn't his thing. "And,

man, that's a great sweater." Tyler was wearing the same black-and-gray striped sweater he'd worn to visit Obama a year earlier. Lori called it "the presidential sweater," and Tyler would wear it again in just eight days.

Clinton and Tyler shook hands and looked each other in the eye. There was even a certain kinship.

"Nice guy," Tyler whispered to me on the way out. "He talked a lot about himself and his stuff."

"Like you, son?"

"Yep."

> Most of us were raised to face failure in the
> face, pick ourselves up, go back to work,
> and make something good happen.
>
> BILL CLINTON, 2013

8

EMPATHY

"He's a Good Kid, Fournier"

Dallas, Texas—*In a cozy reception area, orange leather chairs line the walls beneath pictures of the 43rd president of the United States hosting assorted world leaders at Camp David. Tyler points to former Japanese prime minister Junichiro Koizumi and asks, "Was he an Elvis fan?" I wonder to myself,* How did he know that about Koizumi?

Tyler is 14. He doesn't read newspapers or watch news on TV. I certainly don't talk about my job at home—and yet at some point somebody told him that the Japanese prime minister had an Elvis fixation. Tyler locked it away in a mind that seems to operate like a computer—quick, nimble, and literal. Yes, I reply, he was an Elvis fan.

"He ain't nothing but a hound dog," Tyler says, and laughs.

I see something else in the pictures. They evoke memories

about my years on the road chasing presidential candidates and presidents, a career I loved even as it stole time from my kids and, in two important ways, brought me here to Bush's office. First is the obvious fact that I used my connections to arrange the visit. Second is the painful knowledge that I might have been a better father had I put my family first — had I kept the promise I made Lori when we left Arkansas.

I can't use the job as an excuse. Far more important and busy people keep their priorities in order. I recall a steamy summer day in 1999 when I was at the neighborhood pool with the kids. My cell phone rang. It was Bush, then the governor of Texas and a candidate for president, returning my call about some story that seemed incredibly important at the time. (Now I can't even recall what it was about.) Bush interrupted my first question. "What is all that noise in the background, Fournier?"

"I'm at the pool with my kids, governor."

Bush replied, "Then what the hell are you doing answering your phone?"

Damn good question, sir.

I could be so smug about the ways in which I tried to strike a work-life balance. Like the habit of buying Holly and Gabrielle a doll from every foreign country Clinton and Bush took me to—Bosnia, Britain, China, Chile, Czechoslovakia, France, Germany, Haiti, Hungary, Mexico, Romania, Russia, Spain, Turkey, and so on. I remember sliding my green American Express card across a scuffed wooden counter at a Warsaw store in the late 1990s. "I'll take these," I told the clerk, placing two porcelain blond-wigged dolls on the counter. My cell phone rang.

"When will you be home?" It was Lori. She sounded tired. "I've been up all night crying," she said. The kids were running high fevers. "I don't know what to do."

"Did you call the doctor?"

"Yes. He told me to give them Tylenol and go to the hospital if the fevers don't break by noon."

"What do you want me to do?" That was the wrong question. Lori detected an edge of frustration in my voice. She suspected (correctly) that I was preoccupied with the story I was chasing in Poland—and that at this exact moment I was checking the time to see how far behind her phone calling was putting me. But she didn't know (why would she?) about the familiar internal war I was waging: professional ambition vs. parental guilt. Lori needed me, the kids needed me, and this damn dream job was keeping me away.

"Nothing," Lori snapped. "There's nothing I want you to do." She hung up so loudly that I feared the two White House aides in line behind me had heard it. So I pretended to keep talking.

"I love you, too, babe," I said into a silent cell phone receiver.

As I slunk past the White House aides, both of them young fathers, one of them frowned, shook his head slowly, and softly said, "Been there, Dad."

BUSH GREETED US from behind his neat desk. He was tilted back in his chair with his feet propped on the desktop and a coffee cup marked *POTUS* in his hands. Something about the Texan immediately put Tyler at ease. After a quick handshake, Tyler settled into his chair, striking the same confident, relaxed pose that, with Clinton, had taken him 45 minutes to settle into: hands folded in his lap, fingers intertwined, his legs crossed at the knees.

Bush got down to business. "Going to school?"

"Yes," Tyler replied.

"Do you like school?"

"Pretty good."

"Favorite subject?"

"American studies."

"Do you like to read?"

"Yeah. I read all the time. I don't have a favorite topic."

"Fiction? Nonfiction? Sports?"

"I don't know much about sports."

"Mysteries?"

"I really don't like mysteries."

"Most 14-year-olds don't like to read," Bush said, stretching to compliment Tyler. His conversational style brought to mind a field of Texas oil drills, each one probing, probing, probing, methodically and relentlessly, until hitting pay dirt. "Are your grandparents alive?"

Yes, Tyler said. Before he could continue, I asked Bush about *his* parents. "The aging process is hard to observe," he said, then paused, his smile tight. "And endure." Bush took back the conversation, asking Tyler if he liked to travel.

"As far west as I've been is Las Vegas," Tyler said. "Long story." The short answers bothered me. Were we wasting Bush's time? I interrupted again, reminding Tyler that Clinton had asked him for a favor.

"Oh yeah," Tyler said to Bush. "Bill Clinton sends his best."

Bush smiled warmly. "We've been friends," he said. "We've shared experiences. We're like twins."

Bush said he had a funny story to tell about Clinton—a warm memory that reflected well on the Democrat. But this wasn't a political interview. Pointing to my tape recorder, Bush said, "Turn that off a minute."

MY ACTIONS ON September 11, 2001, the most historic and horrific day of Bush's presidency, exposed a rift between Lori and me and showed me the depths of her sacrifice. I started the day at the White House, pulling a dog-eared index card from my pocket and scanning the list of names and cell phone numbers of my best sources. I punched in a number. Mindy Tucker Fletcher, a longtime aide to Bush who headed the Department of Justice's communications team, picked up

on the first ring. "Turn on CNN," she said. "A plane
has crashed into the World Trade Center."

On the muted TV above my desk, I could see black
smoke swirling from the building. I assumed it was the
work of an errant small-jet pilot. Mindy didn't disagree.

We chatted for eight minutes, until Flight 175
slammed into the South Tower. "Oh my God, did you
see that?" Mindy shouted. I had, but I hadn't processed
it. "Hang on a minute," she said, putting me on hold.

One minute later Mindy was back on the line.
"They think the planes have been hijacked."

"Who thinks?"

"The FBI," she said.

"Let me make sure I've got this right. The FBI be-
lieves the two planes that crashed into the towers in
New York City just now were hijacked?"

"Yes," she said.

"How do you know?"

"Because I'm here, Ron," Mindy said. "The FBI is
right *here*. They've got reports of hijackings." I called
my editor with the bulletin, the first of many that day.

Lori was at home just five miles from the White
House, standing in the kitchen talking to our sister-in-
law, Ingrid. A small TV hung from the cupboard, and
Lori had it on when the second plane hit the towers.
Lori thought, *Boy, they only let idiots fly today.* She hung
up with Ingrid and called me at the White House.

I answered, "Fournier!"

Lori could tell I was frustrated by the interruption from home. "Hi, honey," she said. "Why are these planes flying into these buildings?"

"They were hijacked," I said. "I have to go." Then I hung up. Yes, I hung up on my wife without giving her details I was sharing with the world, without telling her how I would keep myself safe, without even asking about her safety and her plans for the kids, ages 13, 9, and 3, scattered at three separate schools. I was chasing a story. I wanted to win.

Lori set the phone on its cradle and exhaled. She told me later it felt like she had been punched in the stomach. She stared at the TV wondering whether I was in danger. Over and over, the TV showed pictures of the West Wing evacuation, and Lori strained to find me in the fleeing crowd. She didn't know, but I had refused to evacuate because I was too busy reporting and dictating news of the attacks to my editor. It wasn't until 90 minutes later that Lori finally saw me on live TV, slowly walking along an empty White House driveway, the West Wing at my back and a cell phone pressed against my ear. She shouted at the screen, "They evacuated the White House! Why are you in the driveway?"

Years later, while working on this book together, I was still trying to justify to Lori why I was so inattentive on 9/11. "I knew it was a big deal. It was a big story, but it wasn't real life," I told her. "To me, work is almost like a game, and it's not real life. When I come home, whether it's 9/11 or impeachment or whatever, then life begins. I compartmentalize the two."

"Which has upset me the whole time we've been married," Lori interrupted. We had never talked about her feelings before, and my defensiveness had struck a long-buried nerve. "9/11 was a big deal, impeachment was a big deal. I mean, how many times did we say, 'This is the biggest story of your career. No, *this* is the biggest day of your career. Wait, *this* is the biggest story of your career'?" Tears were pooling in the bluest eyes I'll ever see.

"And here I am at home with three kids and you're sometimes my only adult contact for days," Lori continued. "I want to talk about stuff! Because what you're covering is what's happening in the country and it's what everybody is talking about, but you wouldn't talk to me about it. You tell me, 'It's work. I don't want to talk about it.' Okay, let's talk about the diapers I changed and the laundry I did."

Lori didn't sound angry. What I heard (now that I was listening) was humiliation and fear, the nagging sense that the news was more valuable to me than her. "Do you know how small that makes me feel?" she asked. "Do you know how insignificant I felt?"

Truth is, I didn't. I couldn't empathize. Not yet.

BUSH FINISHED HIS off-the-record story about Clinton and I pushed "play" on my digital recorder. He nodded at his inbox, where a shiny baseball and Sharpie sat atop a small pile of papers. "Do you like sports?"

"Hate sports," Tyler said. I winced.

I could feel a burning knot in my belly. Tyler was fending off Bush with one-sentence answers, and I was worried the ex-president would consider him rude or obtuse. I jumped in.

"How about the Rangers and Tigers this year, eh?" I asked.

Bush glared at me and held his palms up as if to say, *Didn't you hear your boy?* I wrote in my notebook, *Stop butting in.* Bush turned back to Tyler and warmly smiled.

"So, Tyler, at 14 this is probably an unfair question to ask, but do you have any idea what you'd like to be when you get older?

"Maybe a comedian."

"Maybe a what?" Bush said, a bit surprised.

"A comedian."

This was the first I'd heard of Tyler's ambition. I had tried to get him to open up, but he never would. I knew what *I* had wanted him to be—a ballplayer— and because of his diagnoses and these guilt trips, I was coming to terms with the fact that my dreams weren't his. But this was new. This was important. This was *amazing.*

"Well," Bush replied, "I'm a pretty objective audience. You might want to try a couple of your lines out on me."

"Nah," Tyler demurred. "I don't have any material."

I told Bush about an improv comedy show on TV that Tyler and I liked to watch together. Then I urged Tyler to tell Bush about the improv class he had just started to take. Tyler shrugged. Bush let him off the hook.

"Ah, interesting," Bush said. "I've met a lot of people. You know how many people ever said, 'I think I'd like to make people laugh'? You're the only guy. That's awesome."

Bush had connected. With an impish smile, he told Tyler about the time that rocker/humanitarian Bono was scheduled to visit the Oval Office. White House aides, knowing their boss was unimpressed by celebrities, worried that Bush would blow it. "[Chief of staff] Josh Bolten comes in and says, 'Now, you know who Bono is, don't you?' Just as he's leaving the Oval Office I said, 'Yeah, he's married to Cher.'"

Bush raised an eyebrow. "Get it?" he asked Tyler. "Bone-o. Bahn-o."

Tyler politely chuckled, and Bush explained the punch line. "It's kind of ironic," he said, "and yet the humor had a point." The point was not to worry about what other people think about you—the perfect lesson for a teenager, particularly one like Tyler who has a hard time fitting in.

"Anyway," Bush continued, "so I'm curious to know, what is an improv class? How does that work?"

"You mostly just practice your improv and make people laugh," Tyler said with a shrug.

Bush played along. "You mostly just stand up in front of people and they throw a subject out and you got to make it humorous?"

"No," Tyler said. "We haven't practiced in front of any audience. It's just like an empty room with a stage."

"But who's watching? The instructor?"

"Yeah." Bush had drawn Tyler out of his shell. This was a more expansive conversation than he typically had with me or even Lori, perhaps because Bush had worked so hard to unearth Tyler's passion. And he wouldn't let go.

"So they say, 'Talk about baseball,' and you have to come up with funny things about baseball?" Bush asked.

I could tell Tyler was excited because the pace of his speech accelerated. "We have, like, these note cards and you have to pick the note cards up and say what's on them."

"In other words, stream of consciousness?" Bush asked.

I told Bush that the class syllabus stresses the importance of eye contact, mutual respect, and the empathy to understand how to play off one another on the fly. These skills come naturally to the young adults in the group. But not to Tyler.

"Very cool," Bush said, turning back to Tyler. "Humor is hard," he said. "You found that?"

"Yes."

"You know why it's hard?" Bush said. "Because the best humor is making fun of yourself, and if you got a big ego, it's hard to make fun of yourself. That's really the best humor in a way, particularly if you're a big shot, you know. It's a wonderful art. That's neat that you're doing that."

BILL CLINTON FAMOUSLY felt the nation's pain. George W. Bush felt Tyler's. While the former Democratic president reads large audiences and parses voting blocs like no other modern politician, his GOP successor reads a room as well as anybody I know.

Bush probed. He listened. He waited until Tyler revealed his hidden passion—then pounced. *Well, I'm a pretty objective audience. You might want to try a couple of your lines out on me.*

It was an example of what Stephen Gray Wallace calls "meeting them where they are"—a form of empathy specific to raising children. You do it literally: bending over and making eye contact. You also do it metaphorically. "Meeting them where they are means accepting them for who they are," said the school psychologist and author who runs CARE, the adolescent research center.

Wallace had a client once, a young man who wouldn't look him in the eye and responded only with one- or two-word answers. Wallace took the boy outside with a Frisbee, and they played catch—silently at first. Over the span of a few weeks, the boy began talking while they played. Wallace met the boy where he was.

Ben Vogelgesang has that certain empathy. We met at Dickey-Stephens Park, home of the Arkansas Travelers minor league baseball team, in North Little Rock, where he was sitting in the front row behind home plate with his 4-year-old son, Gus. Three things stood between them and a 95-mile-per-hour fastball: a squatting catcher, 20 feet of grass and dirt, and a square-mesh protective net that Gus waffled against his face.

"Get your mug away from there, buddy," Ben chuckled. It was boys' night out, a tradition Vogelgesang had started when Gus was just a few months old.

For as long as it took us to finish our beers, Ben and I talked about our marriages, fatherhood, and his son. "Am I his friend? Or am I his superior?" Ben mumbled. "I have no idea of what I'm doing."

I nodded. None of us do.

"So why do you bring him here?" I asked.

"One reason, really," he said. "I love the game. He loves the game. But this is the one place where Gus talks to me."

A few minutes later, I shook hands with Ben and Gus and walked away while the father put his arm around his son's shoulders. Climbing the sticky concrete steps, I could hear Ben probing: "So Mom tells me you're having trouble in school?"

I've seen my niece Anna meet Tyler where he is. They've always had an easy and authentic connection, and Lori thinks that's because Anna lets Tyler be. When they're playing video games, Anna is content to allow Tyler to call the shots. When he wants to play alone, Anna sits in the recliner next to his and quietly reads. He likes having Anna at his side, while at the same time not having to engage with her. She's not a threat to him. She's not a source of pressure upon him. Yet her presence makes Tyler less lonely.

What did Anna's example teach me? The power of acceptance—and presence. While wrapping up this book, I ended the habit of interrupting Tyler's quiet time in our basement, where he reads, watches comedians on the Internet, or plays video games. Rather than announcing myself with a forced "Let's talk," I began a new routine: I now come downstairs without fanfare and slip into the recliner abutting his, pull out a book or a newspaper, and quietly read.

Tyler almost always smiles and nods his head. Sometimes he'll give me a "Hi, Dad!"—with the practiced enthusiasm of an evolving Aspie. Then we sit quietly, together.

OUR HOUR WAS UP. Tyler had been terse, maybe even rude, but Bush was solicitous. Rather than fight Tyler's idiosyncrasies, he rolled with them, exactly as he had in the Oval Office nine years earlier. He responded to every clipped answer with another probing question. Bush, a man who famously doesn't suffer fools or breaches of propriety, gave my son the benefit of the doubt. I was beginning to think that many people are more perceptive and less judgmental toward Tyler than his own father. Bush certainly was.

He thanked Tyler for coming, and came from behind his desk to show us out. He invited us to tour a nearby warehouse housing artifacts awaiting the construction of his presidential library. There was more small talk; I think we chatted a bit about bike racing and journalism before Tyler walked out of the office a step or two ahead of me. Outside of Tyler's earshot, Bush shook my hand, squinted in that way he does, and said, "He's a good kid, Fournier."

"I know." It was an honest answer. He's a good kid, which makes him a happy kid, which makes me a decent dad—almost worthy of my brilliantly unique son.

The best humor is making fun of yourself, and if you got a big ego, it's hard to make fun of yourself.

GEORGE W. BUSH, FEBRUARY 2012

9

ACCEPTANCE

"I Had Her Back"

Falls Church, Virginia—*Tyler and I are sitting in the car outside a bookstore. The Barnes & Noble in northern Virginia is where we spend many hours, sharing our love of books and time alone. He's reading an early draft of this story. His story.*

"It's okay," my little professor says. "But it's a bit of a cliché." He asks me to say he's no longer afraid of bees or of the dark. He instructs me to delete a passage in which I tell him, "Courage isn't the absence of fear. It's overcoming your fears." It must be a misquotation, Tyler says, because his father doesn't talk so eloquently. And he's not impressed with my original conclusion.

Fair enough, I say. "So help me find a better ending. What did you get out of the project, pal?"

"All I got out of it was time with you," he laughs. "No

offense." I tell Tyler there's got to be a better way to end our story than saying we spent time together. "This isn't Twilight," he says, referring to the film saga he wouldn't be caught dead watching. "This is you and me. Just write that we like to spend time together. That's a big deal for a kid like me."

It would be a big deal for me—if I believed him. The fact is, I know that time with me isn't his first preference. He'd rather be alone, and I can accept that now. But Tyler is telling me what he knows I want to hear, and he's doing something he'd really rather not do. That's progress for an Aspie.

Thanks to the team Lori put together, Tyler is learning to connect and to belong. And thanks to the project she created for us, I saw that progress firsthand. Tyler will be a happy, thriving adult. I might have even helped. Being with him—accepting him, watching him overcome his fears, and seeing him through the forgiving eyes of others—this is my field of dreams. I don't need to "have a catch" with Tyler to be a good father; I simply need to let him be. Rather than sweat over his Asperger's, I now realize how much I'd miss if he wasn't an Aspie—his humor, his bluntness, his joyful obsessions with everything from video games to his family. His unique wiring comes with almost no ego; not even the presidential visits seemed to affect Tyler's sense of self. As the rest of society seems to be perfecting irony and affectation, my boy is constitutionally unable to bullshit. God, I love him. And now I know others will love him, too.

On the trips to Arkansas and Texas, I saw through both presidents a successful future for Tyler—through Clinton, big

possibilities for a boy with a sharp mind and rough edges;
through Bush, Tyler's gift of humor as a means to find con-
fidence in himself and connections with others. In the Oval
Office years ago, I thought Bush had ordered me to "love that
boy" in spite of his idiosyncrasies. Now, I realize, I love my
son because of them.

This is what I tried to tell Tyler in the car outside the
bookstore. "I get it, Dad," he said dismissively. "Now can we
go home? I want to play video games."

"Is THIS THING on?" Tyler, now 16, tapped the cor-
rugated silver microphone, mimicking the professional
comedians we had watched and heard together since
the Bush visit two years earlier. The crowd tittered as
he nervously shuffled his feet. "Hi, I'm Tyler, Bompa's grandson." Using the kids' nickname for my father, Tyler introduced himself to dozens of family and
friends gathered for lunch at a church hall just north of
Detroit. We were eating simple food—roast beef and
chicken, if memory serves—and choosing from three
brands of beer, including Dad's favorite, Labatt's Blue.

When Tyler launched into his story, the clattering
and clanging of lunch stopped, as did every conversation. "When I was a kid, we would go to Erie House
and all of us would play on the tire swing out front by
the lake," Tyler said, referring to the cottage on Lake

Erie where Dad once played hockey with his kids and their pals. "One day I asked Bompa where the tire came from. He said, 'Oh, it washed up from the lake.'

"The way my mind is wired," Tyler went on, "I thought he meant the whole truck was at one point hanging from the tree and it fell into the lake—and the only thing left on the rope was that tire."

While the crowd laughed, I turned to Lori in the seat next to me and saw her tearing up. We were overwhelmed at the sight of our socially challenged son giving a public speech—and embracing his autism: *the way my mind is wired.* For the friends and family in the room, there had been a time, not that long ago, when they didn't know what to make of Tyler. They didn't know how to connect. They may have even been a little hurt by his perceived rudeness.

But with his diagnosis came acceptance. In the last three years, we've noticed more family trying to engage him—not pushing him exactly, but going out of their way to listen. Although family members sometimes have a hard time understanding Tyler, they now hear him, because they know how important they are to him. Which is why it meant so much to watch Tyler share a favorite memory with these loving people. The setting made it all the more poignant: It was my dad's wake.

THERE IS SOME comfort in the discovery that I am not alone. I found scores of other parents struggling along the path to acceptance, where love and fear and self-regard blind us to the subtle difference between guiding and pushing our children. "The easy part of parenting is the dreams we have for our kids; we all have them," Lori told me one night near the end of the guilt trips. "The hard part, the goal of all this, is learning to accept and love the kids you have."

Stacey and Adam Bromberg now recognize that Gavin is a good kid, a happy kid with "a good group of friends" and a bright future. "I want to say that he'll succeed in computers after going to college or landing a job even before he goes to college. He loves computers," Stacey said. "I definitely see success in his future, no matter what."

Mitch Dworkin is married and happy, still making progress on his issues with Asperger's and hoarding, which is a symptom of his obsessive-compulsive disorder. He calls his father "my best friend." Reverence is the best word to describe how Alan Dworkin describes his son. "The kid gets kicked in the head and gets back up. Kicked and kicked and kicked, and he just won't give up. It may be the most courageous thing I've ever witnessed, that boy."

John S., the father I met over beers in Lansing, Michigan, is working less and spending more time with his boy. "Luckily, we found a public school with staff willing and able to help him, and counseling, and he is working his way through the first grade," John said. "I am incredibly proud of him and growing more so I come to fully understand the hurdles he faces."

Megan Chung didn't get into Harvard. It was her only rejection. "I just got back from visiting Princeton a couple of days ago and I could not be more enthused to call the place home," she emailed me just as this book was being completed. "Personally, I think it's a better fit for me than Harvard."

But this isn't just about Megan, is it?

"My mother was excited for all of my college acceptances (including Columbia, Brown, Cornell, and Duke), so much so that I think Harvard's rejection was just a shrug and an 'oh well' to her."

Not all stories come with a happy ending. Remember my basketball pal Scott Gilbride? Rather than shirk from Mary Lacey's depression, Scott and his wife, Anne, fought it like a cancer. So did Mary Lacey. She tried therapy, intense exercise, modified diets, and even the medication that Scott despised. The Gilbrides threw everything at their daughter's depression.

It was not enough. One day recently, Mary Lacey killed herself. "I'm sorry I can't take the pain any longer," she wrote to her family. "No longer will I watch my suffering affect my family. You all won't have to deal with the ups and downs anymore. I love you." After thanking her father, mother, both sisters, and several friends for their love and support, Mary Lacey divided up her possessions, giving them away to family and friends: a racing bike, a David Yurman ring, Michael Kors eyeglasses, a Marc Jacobs bag, weightlifting shoes, her grandmother's ring, and her laptop, the one she used to write her last note. "Please remember that this was my decision and no one's fault," Mary Lacey wrote. "I have the best family I could have ever wanted and I don't want to keep hurting you with my depression."

This is any parent's worst nightmare. A child's suicide is not something a mother or father wants to ever accept. And yet I think Scott and Anne found some peace in understanding that what happened to Mary Lacey was out of their control. Maybe even out of Mary Lacey's control.

Her funeral filled the seats and side aisles at St. Mary's Catholic Church in Alexandria, Virginia. Eulogists recalled Mary Lacey's loud laugh, her fierce competitiveness, and her selfless knack for making everybody feel better in her presence. Nobody shrank from the cause of death: depression. The Catholic priest who spoke at her funeral, Father James Greenfield, asked family and friends to not judge Mary Lacey or her parents. Given the Catholic Church's firm teachings against suicide, Greenfield's homily was an extraordinary act of forgiveness, grace, and acceptance. "Hers was a medical problem," he said, "not a moral one."

FOR LORI AND me, that road to acceptance of Tyler's issues began in Dr. Quinn's office, with the autism diagnosis. A label we once feared actually opened doors to a vast variety of services. It also helped the people around Tyler to better understand him. Finally, and most important, the diagnosis helped Tyler better understand himself.

He likes to say, "When you've met a person with Asperger's, you've met *one person* with Asperger's." His point: While autism is an important part of his identity, it will not define him.

Tyler embraces the theory of *neurodiversity,* defined by author Steve Silberman as "the notion that conditions like autism, dyslexia, and attention-deficit/hyperactivity disorder (ADHD) should be regarded as naturally occurring cognitive variations with distinctive strengths that have contributed to the evolution of technology and culture, rather than mere checklists of deficits and dysfunctions."

Ask Tyler about being an Aspie, and he'll give you a list of successful men and women who succeeded not *despite of* autism, but *because of* it. "The notion that the cure for the most disabling aspects of autism will never be found in a pill but in supportive communities is one that parents have been coming to on their own for generations," Silberman writes in *NeuroTribes: The Legacy of Autism and the Future of Neurodiversity.*

Lori and I didn't run away from the diagnosis. We ran *toward* it, building a support system for Tyler. We started with his education, which had stalled at Williamsburg Middle School, a large and impersonal public school catering to affluent families in the Washington suburb of Arlington, Virginia. While teachers focused on the highest achievers, Tyler's grades suffered, and he was increasingly ostracized and bullied. His attention-deficit issues had qualified Tyler for special services since the second grade, but Williamsburg officials were stingy with their accommodations.

Not only did Dr. Quinn tell us to fight for Tyler, she taught us how. Go to the next special-needs meeting with a list of specific accommodations that Tyler requires, she said. Things like a laptop, more in-class assistance, and social skills training. "If they raise any objections or fail to accommodate Tyler in every way," she said, "ask them this: 'So you're telling me that you can't educate my son?'" That is the trigger, she said— the magic sentence—that tells school administrators you are prepared to yank your kids (and their federal money) out of the district.

Game on. Two weeks later, Lori and I attended the annual review of Tyler's special-needs program linked to his ADD diagnosis. We brought with us Quinn's 30-page report that had just labeled Tyler an Aspie. The special-education team quickly accepted her findings, but they hemmed and hawed over our request for new accommodations, until I took a deep breath and said, "So you're telling me that you can't educate my son?" The county's special-education director looked at the assistant principal and raised an eyebrow. "No, we're not saying that," she said. "But we are here to tell you there is a new program opening at H-B Woodlawn next year that caters specifically to boys like Tyler: kids with high-intellect Asperger's."

H-B Woodlawn is a county-run magnet school with a waiting list so long that children must win a lottery to enroll. Serving grades 6–12, the school has an enrollment of just 600—half the size of Williamsburg. Located just two miles east of our home, H-B gives students more freedom and responsibility than the typical school, with an open campus, liberal dress code, college-style schedules, and a tradition of the students calling teachers by their first names.

The kids are encouraged to embrace their inner quirkiness. Different is cool at H-B. School principal Frank Haltiwanger fostered a culture of tolerance that extends from the most popular kids to the nerdiest. At one graduation ceremony, the principal called out the names of two students, a boy and a girl, who were leaving H-B for other schools. With his arms casually draped over the departing kids' shoulders, the principal said, "Now, we all hope these two are welcomed into their new schools, right? We want their new classmates to invite them into their cliques, and to their parties, and to stand up for them if anybody acts against them, right?"

Every head nodded. The two kids were well liked. "Okay then, next year we will have 10 new students coming to H-B from other schools," Frank continued. "I expect you to invite them into your cliques, and to your parties, and to stand up for them if anybody acts against them. That's the H-B way."

Sitting in the back of the room, Lori whispered to me that Frank was the perfect principal for kids like Tyler. I told her that Frank had instilled a culture of community and competence throughout the staff and student body. "He may be the best leader in Washington."

A few months after enrolling in H-B for seventh grade, Tyler decided to enter a talent show. He wanted to do a stand-up comedy act, an idea that scared the hell out of me. What if kids laughed *at* him rather than with him? The weekend before the show, Tyler and I cribbed jokes from the Internet and practiced his routine. It was rough. Tyler talked too fast and had chosen jokes that made him laugh. He was more concerned about his own amusement than that of his audience— exactly what you'd expect from an Aspie. Come showtime, his first two jokes bombed, but the kids applauded politely. That gave Tyler confidence. He slowed his cadence and looked audience members in the eye. They laughed, cheered, chanted Tyler's name, and later voted him the second-place winner.

Wiping away a tear, I turned to the nearest teacher and said, "You're not just teaching these kids how to read and write. You're teaching them to be good citizens, aren't you?" The teacher shrugged, smiled, and said, "That's what you pay us for." For a cynical reporter who makes his living documenting the failure of national institutions, this was one hell of a moment. *That's what you pay us for.*

For the handful of students who happened to be Aspies, H-B offered social skills classes staffed by Asperger's specialists. They worked out of a small classroom decorated with large, overstuffed couches and chairs—part of an effort to create a zone of safety and comfort, where the students could unwind from a day of socializing that for most kids is refreshing and fun but for Aspies is utterly exhausting.

In time, Tyler made friends outside the Asperger's program. He was part of a small group of quirky boys who were equally obsessed with video games and who ate lunch together in the school hallways. We tried for months to get the boys over to our house or out somewhere together after school. Finally, they agreed to go to a movie. I drove them to the theater and reported back to Lori that, despite our fears, they *really* liked Tyler and were *actual* friends. One of my happiest moments as a dad occurred that night, when Tyler burst into the house to tell his mom, "Me and my friends are home!"

Recently, we got a note from Tyler's first Asperger's aide telling us about a holiday party in which 30 kids and teachers gathered in the hallway to do the electric slide. "My heart was so happy to see Tyler dancing with the group," she wrote. "He had a big smile on his face! I couldn't stop watching him."

Don't tell me schools are just for learning. After a few months, Tyler declared H-B Woodlawn to be "a life-changing experience."

OUTSIDE H-B, LORI built and managed a team of professionals, including a psychiatrist to manage his drugs and an Asperger's therapist to work with the school team. In addition, he attended a weekly therapy group with a mix of troubled teens. Some had issues with drugs or the judicial system. Others were constantly fighting with their parents. Tyler slowly learned how to listen to his peers, show empathy, and express his innermost feelings. Most people could benefit from a simple sharpening of these social skills. For an Aspie like Tyler, the challenge is akin to learning a foreign language.

Not too long ago, a girl in the group announced that she was no longer attending the program. Tyler told his mom that he would miss her. To parents of a typical child, that would be no big deal. For us, it was a double breakthrough: Tyler had grown close enough to a person to miss her, *and* he was able to tell us about his feelings.

The next week, Tyler arrived for the group session and sat by himself in the waiting room. Lori knew to sit far apart from her teenager. She told me later, "A couple other kids in his group came in and were talking to each other. Then one of them called over to Ty and said, 'What do you think, Tyler? Come on over here.' Ty got up, walked over, and joined their conversation. I thought I was going to cry. I could not look at them."

A week after that, a middle-aged woman was loudly mocking eating disorders and Asperger's in the therapist's waiting room. One of the girls in Tyler's group walked over to the lady and politely asked her to stop. "I have an eating disorder," the girl said. Tyler followed his companion over. "And I have Asperger's," he said.

Later, I told him how proud I was that he would stand up for himself and his friend. "That was the right and good thing to do," I said.

Tyler shrugged. "I had her back."

Then there was Holly's wedding reception. Actually, it was the after-party at Tom's bar, where Tyler broke out of his shell as soon as the dance floor opened. Lori and I hadn't realized that one of the things Tyler does in our basement is watch and memorize music videos, nor did we know that the kid can *really* dance. I don't have the words to describe the joy I felt watching my son confidently perform—often solo, as family and friends cheered, but also, and more important, while pulling friends and family into his orbit.

There were so many other *big* small moments. Like the day he ran up the stairs from the basement to declare, "I've got to take a shower!" It was his first unprompted act of hygiene. Or the first time he did his homework without Lori's help, a tenth-grader telling his mom, "I got this." Like many Aspies, he is essentially a handful of years behind typical teenagers in social and personal development. On his own initiative, Tyler now brushes his teeth, makes his bed, takes his medicine, and goes to sleep. You might wonder why these things are worth celebrating. The reason is because there was a time, not too long ago, when we didn't know whether Tyler could be independent. Now there's little doubt that he will be.

Even as I finish this final chapter, we're seeing progress. Tyler told his therapist recently that he was feeling "a little jumpy." It turned out he hadn't taken his medicine, and the fact that he noticed a change in his chemical makeup is a big deal. The same day, Tyler told his mom that he didn't want to go to the Winter Classic hockey game with me and his sisters, but he knew that Holly and Gabrielle wanted it to be a family affair. "Can you believe that he's putting himself in the girls' shoes?" Lori happily asked me. Yes, I can.

Three years after his visit with Bush, Tyler still does something remarkable every Saturday afternoon: He walks onstage at a comedy club near our home and performs improv with a group of adults. It's one thing to crack a joke; it's another to make one up on the spot—to follow the other players' subtle verbal and nonverbal clues and to collectively create a skit. It's a social function so complex that most neurotypical people would freeze or flail. Not my boy.

The biggest issue is still friendship. That movie with the boys occurred two years ago, and Tyler hasn't had an outing with them since then. They still hang out together at school, but something is blocking Tyler from making connections beyond H-B. He has his companions at group therapy and colleagues in improv—sincere, strong relationships within the limits of those activities. But he does not have friends in the traditional sense, which worries Lori and me. Will Tyler start making friends? Will he be lonely? Will he define friendship differently than his parents do? He'd tell you, "I'm working on that."

LORI IS WORKING on her own happiness after years of sacrificing it for mine—and for our kids. She graduated a year ahead of me from the University of Detroit (now University of Detroit Mercy) and we married less than a year after my graduation. Rather than leverage her degree for a public relations job in Michigan, Lori climbed into a rental van the morning after our wedding and moved to Arkansas, where I had found a newspaper job and she had no prospects.

I took our only car to work every day, which meant

Lori had to walk a mile to the nearest mall to apply for jobs. She found work as a bookstore clerk, and gave birth to Holly and Gabrielle while climbing the ranks to store manager. When we moved to Little Rock to further my career, Lori took over the state's biggest bookstore, a freestanding Waldenbooks frequented by then Governor Bill Clinton.

Before Tyler was born, when the girls were little and we still lived in Arkansas, I had a pretty good work-life balance. That changed in 1993, when Clinton was elected president and the Associated Press transferred me to Washington, a huge and exciting career boost. I promised Lori that my job would always come second to her and the kids.

In Washington, Lori stayed with Waldenbooks and was given command of two stores, one in northern Virginia and another in tony Georgetown. She was on track to be a district manager—and Lord knows what else. Her job wasn't any easier or less important than mine, and yet the burden of feeding, clothing, transporting, and in all ways raising the kids largely fell to Lori. I might drop the girls off at the sitter or school, but I rarely was available to pick them up. I missed dinner with Lori and the kids more often than I made it. I took every other trip with Clinton—and the president traveled *a lot*. The job came first, family second.

One day, on sleet-glazed city streets, Lori left work

at the mall to pick up Holly from kindergarten, where she attended an after-school program that closed at 6:00 p.m. Heavy traffic delayed Lori's arrival until 6:10. "You're late," the program coordinator snapped at Lori. "If you can't be here by six o'clock, we are going to expel your child from extended day."

Years later, Lori told me how angry and ashamed she was. "That lady made me feel like I didn't give a rat's ass about whether Holly was going to get out of day care, and of course I worried all day long." After that incident, Lori resigned as manager to work part-time, and a few months later abandoned her career entirely. We put my work over hers, and me over her.

"I didn't think I was a great mom. I felt a little worthless," she said. "I was always a good housekeeper—that I know. I can remember going to pick up the girls at elementary school and not getting dressed or doing my hair. That sounds superficial, but I would literally be in sweats and I would hide in the car. I didn't want to see anybody. I didn't want to see the other moms. I guess I was sort of going through some depression, and I would tell the kids, 'I'll be parked on the road. Walk down and find me.'"

Trust me: Lori is a great wife and mother. Still, she felt the other mothers were better than her. They seemed to be busier outside the home—some balanced careers, and others had family schedules crammed with events. "I avoided that, which explains why I don't have a big circle of friends to this day," Lori said.

Personal insecurities and the anxieties of mothering a young boy with social issues forced her into a shell, where she could protect herself and Tyler from failure and embarrassment. She pulled away from friends. She kept family and acquaintances at arm's length. She was desperately lonely.

SOMETHING SHIFTED FOR the better after Tyler's diagnosis. Lori gained confidence, proud of what she has accomplished on his behalf.

"This thing with Tyler hasn't changed my social circle or restarted my career, but it has given me a purpose," Lori said. "It has made me feel more competent as a person. It's very complicated taking care . . ." She paused. "I'm going to cry."

Then: "It's very complicated taking care of Tyler. There are a lot of balls in the air all the time with the different therapies that he needs and the schoolwork that he has to get done, because as he grows . . . it gets harder."

In 2010, shortly after Tyler's diagnosis, I left my dream job at the Associated Press to become editor in chief of a news organization that guaranteed me more time and flexibility for family matters. Lori wanted me home more. The *National Journal Group* team was true to its word, but I found running a newsroom to be demanding under even the best of circumstances. After the 2012 presidential election, I stepped down as editor in chief and became a columnist—the most family-friendly job I've ever had.

With Holly in Detroit, Gabrielle in Lansing, and our extended families planted in lower Michigan, Lori and I made plans to leave Washington and move to our home state after Tyler graduates from high school in June 2016. Family first, for once.

For her next act, Lori has talked about consulting for parents of special-needs children. There's an incredible need, and she'd be terrific—some other families' hero.

IN THE SPRING of 2014, my father died. The cause of death was Lewy-body dementia, an insidious disease that rapidly robs its victims of both mind and body. So little is known about Lewy-body that it's often misdiagnosed as Parkinson's. Mom decided to rent a boat and scatter Dad's ashes in the Detroit River, where it feeds into our beloved Lake Erie.

We boarded in St. Clair Shores and filled the 30-minute ride with awkward conversation—the kind of chitchat you hear in the first hour of a holiday gathering, before the alcohol kicks in. *How's the job? How are the kids? How about those Tigers?* We spoke little about Dad; that's what the wake had been for, I guess. We spoke nothing of the tension over his care and the secrecy around it.

My sister, Raquel, was the first to lose her composure, dashing to the deck below to find a bathroom.
She almost ran into Tyler at the bottom of the stairs,
where he was sitting alone. He recognized her distress,
jumped to his feet, and said, "I don't know what to
say to make you feel better, but I can give you a hug,"
That was exactly what she needed. "He hugged me so
tight. And kept hugging me," Raquel told me later. "It
meant the world to me."

When we arrived at the appointed spot, the boat
stopped and we made our way to the bow. Raquel
took Dad's ashes from our mother and poured them
over the side, while Mom stood alone behind her. My
brothers made eye contact with me. *What should we do?*
Rather than step forward to comfort Mom, I took two
steps back. It was not my finest hour.

But my son—well, Tyler exceeded my greatest expectations, stepping in front of his father and his uncles to hold his grandmother tightly in a one-arm hug.
He leaned down and whispered in her ear. "Everyone
thinks I'm comforting you," he told her with a smile,
"but really I need comforting."

Now, finally, I know what perfect is. It's a child
blessed with the grace to show goodness, even on the
worst of days. No, Tyler is not my idealized son. He is
my ideal one.

> I would rather have this book published than
> anything that has ever been written about me.
>
> **THEODORE ROOSEVELT, TO THE EDITOR OF**
> *THEODORE ROOSEVELT'S LETTERS TO HIS*
> *CHILDREN,* **SHORTLY BEFORE HIS DEATH**

HISTORY LESSONS

Among America's most accomplished men, U.S. presidents foundered as fathers. Their children exhibited higher-than-average rates of divorce, alcoholism, and premature death. "Many children of high achievers struggle with feelings of abandonment and take more time in life to establish their own separate identity," wrote historian Doug Wead in *All the Presidents' Children*. "But this seems especially true for the sons of presidents, particularly those sons who worked for their fathers in the White House, or who were the firstborn, or who bore the same name, sons who were in some way considered to be 'in line' for the presidency themselves. It seems that the closer a male child was to the parents, the more likely he would be to self-destruct."

For the rest of us, there is hope.

I'm no expert, but I know a few, starting with several child development professionals who helped me contextualize my research and reading, and including more than three dozen parents who related their experiences, insights, and advice. When parents get together, they tend to talk about their kids and their challenges. They're not just bitching; they're sharing—sharing hard-won wisdom and advice. In that tradition, here are a few closing thoughts:

Don't parent for the future; parent for today. Most of the pressure we impose upon our kids comes from worry about what's around the corner. Can I get him into a good preschool? Can she play travel soccer? How many friends will he have? What kind of a guy will she marry?

Tomorrow will come. Don't rush it.

A couple of tips for parenting in the present. First, create small moments. One weekend at a time, over the course of several years, I took my kids to every park in our county. I kept a wrinkled map in the glove box that we used to locate area parks and give them our own special nicknames ("House Park" was my favorite). When the girls were little, I told bedtime stories that I made up on the fly, with goofy characters and wild storylines. And while I put work ahead of family too often, I rarely missed birthdays, ball games, recitals, and other special events.

Second, treasure every moment. Make memories.

I jotted notes on the memorable outings and conversations I had with my kids. I took mental pictures. I would literally say to myself, "Don't forget this, Ron." And I won't.

Guide, don't push. There is a world of difference between dancing in the living room with your daughter and forcing her to take ballet classes. The first approach is a playful and authentic way to expose her to a potential hobby. The second is conflating your dreams with hers. Remember, Goldilocks parents are involved and responsive. They set high expectations but respect their kids' autonomy.

"I'm a firm believer in supporting our kids in what they want to do rather than fulfill our own expectations," said Lynn Schofield Clark, author of *The Parenting App*. We spoke at length about how she tries to shift the burden of expectations and responsibility from her shoulders to those of her children. For instance, she didn't intervene when her 16-year-old son talked online with his girlfriend past midnight during the holidays. The next day, however, she told him he was too tired and crabby to go mountain climbing. "I tried to show that the choices were about him, not me," Clark said. "My role as a parent is to be more of a guide than a dictator."

Don't beat yourself up. The knock on families today is that narcissistic, overinvolved parents are producing spoiled, entitled children with no values. While there may be some truth to the conventional wisdom, reality is more complicated. In *The Price of Privilege*, Madeline Levine said kids are troubled, not spoiled. Parents are struggling, not self-indulgent. The struggles of families are real, not trivial—and most parents feel alone and unanchored. "Anxious parents," Levin wrote, "make anxious children."

This means you're not alone. Relax. Do your best. Don't wallow in guilt. That may seem like odd advice from a guy who writes about so-called guilt trips. In *Dad Is Fat,* comedian Jim Gaffigan captures the absurdity of self-serious parenting. "I feel guilty when I travel out of town to do shows," he wrote. "I feel guilty when I'm in town and I don't spend every single moment with my children. I feel guilty when I'm spending time with my children and I am not doing something constructive toward their intellectual development. I feel guilty when I feed them the unhealthy food they like. I feel guilty when I drop them off at school. I feel guilty when I pick them up at school. I feel guilty mostly for writing this book instead of spending time with them. Great, now I've probably made you feel guilty for reading this book. I feel guilty about that now, too. Sorry."

Celebrate all victories. The first time Tyler took a shower without prompting or did his homework without complaining—those were *big* small things. Your son gets his first passing grade in math. Your daughter cleans up her room without being asked. Big deals? Heck yes. There are no small victories in parenting. Only victories.

I learned this from the mother of a severely autistic boy from rural Maryland. Sitting at a mall coffee shop, the woman told me that her backyard is a haven for rabbits. Her son never paid attention to them. Never noticed them. Until one day she heard him shouting and found him pointing at a rabbit outside the kitchen window. "He wanted me to come look at it. It was one of those moments, a breakthrough," she sobbed. "You might shrug, but it was a big deal."

Slow down. "Contemporary hyper-parenting is a true product of our times—manufactured in a high-tech environment, according to a set of stratospherically high expectations," wrote Dr. Alvin Rosenfeld and Nicole Wise in *The Overscheduled Child*. "The emphasis on perfection and perpetual motion is destroying family life."

Their advice is simple. Limit your activities. Give yourself a break. Don't spend money on products that distract you, appease your child, or further complicate your life. Finally (and ironically), "be discriminating about the advice you pay attention to."

Make different cool. When my siblings and I got old enough to get into trouble, my father had a saying: "It's cool to be different." It was his way of giving us the courage to defy peer pressure. *When everybody else seems to be skipping school, it's cool to be different. When* *everybody else is smoking dope at a party, be the one cool enough to say, "No thanks."*

As a parent, I see his advice in a different light: Tyler is cool *because* he's different. Rather than be ashamed of whatever makes your children different, embrace that uniqueness.

Be a spouse first, a parent second. The best thing I did for my kids was loving their mom. (Granted, loving Lori is the easiest thing I'll ever do.)

The typical child will live with his or her parents for 18 to 25 years. A fortunate couple will be married at least twice as long, and their commitment to each other can be a model for their children. It's like my dad told me when I was starting my family: "As much as I loved you guys, I never forgot that you would grow up and be gone, and I'd always be with your mom."

In *The Overscheduled Child*, Rosenfeld and Wise broaden the logic to stress the importance of prioritizing your family. "Our children are with us for a short time before they head out into their own lives, busy with friends, college, jobs, and eventually their own families. We ought to enjoy them, and the brief flicker of time we have with them," they wrote. "Family life should not be overloaded with chores and commitments that add unnecessary resentment to daily life."

Share even the bad news. My brother Tim recently asked me, with regard to Tyler, "How can siblings, classmates, and other peers be made to understand and retool their interactions?" The question scratches at the feelings of love and helplessness that are conjured when a child is in trouble. The most important thing is communication. While we were slow to get Tyler diagnosed, we immediately shared the results with family and friends. The benefits of that decision were twofold. First, the most important people in our lives were able to help us. Second, the information helped them. They had known Tyler was struggling, but they didn't know how much or why—and certainly didn't want to risk offending us by asking. The diagnosis gave our families and friends the green light to do what families and friends want to do: love us and help us.

Fight for your kids. Lori and I will always be indebted to Dr. Quinn for giving us the language we needed to squeeze more services out of our public school for Tyler. I hope in some small measure this book inspires parents to seek the help they need.

For many parents, however, the hurdles are far higher than they were for Lori and me. Their kids go to poorer schools. They can't afford private services. They don't have networks of family and friends to help pick up the slack. This is where Hillary Clinton was right: It takes a village to raise a child, which means every taxpayer must be willing to support public services for children, especially those with special needs. Federal, state, and local governments must invest in child welfare, and spend the money with efficiency and transparency. Business leaders must view child welfare budgets as a down payment on their future workforce. Elderly residents must support child services that they'll no longer need. Charities and nonprofit organizations must spend less on overhead and more on their stated purposes.

Finally, we parents can't wait for information and services to come to us. We can't use obstacles as excuses. We can't be perfect, but we can always do better.

Channel your inner Aspie. What makes Tyler and other people with Asperger's syndrome unique also makes them a model for the rest of us. Their hyperliteral mind-sets make honesty as much a part of their nature as breathing. Tyler is almost incapable of being duplicitous or hypocritical. Lori says, "Nobody rats himself out quite like Tyler." Every day when he comes home from school, Lori will ask, "Do you have homework?" Tyler replies, "No"—then pauses for a heartbeat, bows his shoulders, and mumbles, "Yes."

While he has a hard time expressing empathy, Tyler may be one of the most caring people I know other than his mom. I think there is something about living so deeply inside their heads that make Tyler and fellow Aspies extraordinarily sensitive to the effects of isolation, criticism, and other slights—even if they're less attuned than normal to when and how they might be negatively affecting somebody else.

It's easy to get hung up on the traits Aspies struggle with: inflexible and rigid thinking, making connections and generalizations, complex problem solving, abstract thinking, multitasking, and the social issues that Tyler tackled on our trips. It's important to value and model the traits that author Liane Holliday Willey called "20 first-rate ways to describe Aspies."

---

1. Very loyal
2. Open and honest
3. Guardians of those less able
4. Detail oriented
5. Uninterested in social politics
6. Often witty and entertaining
7. Capable of developing very strong "splinter skills" (savant-level abilities in an area of intense interest)
8. Storage bank for facts and figures
9. Tenacious researchers and thinkers
10. Logical
11. Enthusiastic about their passionate interests
12. Able to create beautiful images in their mind's eye
13. Finely tuned in to their sensory systems
14. Ethical and principled
15. Dependable
16. Good at word games and wordplay
17. Inquisitive
18. Rule followers
19. Unambiguous
20. Average to above-average intelligence

Do you see your child reflected in Willey's rich list of adjectives? I bet you do. In his or her own way, every child is lucky enough to be different.

I can't count the reasons I love my boy. I used to say I hope to be worthy of Tyler. Now I see that I should hope to be more like him.

ACKNOWLEDGMENTS

In December 2012, I published an essay in *National Journal* magazine titled "First, Family: How Two Presidents Helped Me Deal with Guilt, Love, and Fatherhood." A cable news network invited me to discuss the story on TV, and I remember the scene inside a crowded green room: Several guests and an equal number of college interns buzzed around a coffee maker and pastry plate. Every few minutes, an intern announced the name of their assigned guest, offering an escort to the studio.

I was the last guest summoned. My assigned intern was a shy 22-year-old who wordlessly walked me into the studio— then stood waiting for me when my segment was over. He led me to an empty elevator and pushed the "lobby" button. As soon as we were alone, the intern stepped to my side of the compartment, looked me in the eyes, shook my hand, and said, "Thank you for coming on our show." I thought it was a gracious gesture, if not a bit awkward.

When the elevator opened, I started to say good-bye. The young man interrupted. "I want to tell you something," he blurted. "I have Asperger's syndrome. Thank you for writing the story and please let me know if I can help Tyler at all."

I can't tell you the intern's name because he asked me not to share it; autism can carry an unfortunate stigma. But I owe him this thank you—for being the first to tell me how much Tyler's story mattered to Aspies; for his willingness to help my son; and for his time as a source and sounding board for the book that grew out of the *National Journal* story.

There are so many others to thank, starting of course with Lori—my bride, my muse, and my greatest friend. Who else?

Tyler, who had the authority to veto this project at every stage. We love that boy.

Our girls. Holly's tenacious and thorough editing spared her dad great embarrassment. Gabrielle's wise words of encouragement helped me see the project through others' eyes. We love these young women.

George W. Bush, Bill Clinton, Barack and Michelle Obama, and their associates, including Doug Band, Elizabeth Bibi, Nelson Chenault, Freddy Ford, Karen Hughes, Jordan Johnson, Alan Lowe, Lena Moore, Skip Rutherford, and Doug Sosnik. These public servants "pay it forward" in many ways that go unnoticed.

My siblings (Tim, Mike, and Raquel), extended family, and many friends who keep drawing us back to Michigan. My mother, who encouraged me to write honestly, if painfully. My father, whose interview for this book became the spine of his obituary. "I had a great wife," he told me. "I had a great life with her."

Lori's family, particularly her sister Pam and our niece Anna, who forged a special connection with Tyler. Her father, Larry, brother, Craig, and cousins, Karen and Kris, who also call us back to Michigan.

Our heroes at H-B Woodlawn, including Leigh Buckley-Altice, Krista Rivera, and since-retired principal Frank Haltiwanger. Cynthia Evans, Tyler's tutor, who made math bearable. Karen Ready, who taught Tyler in third grade and was the first educator to really "get" him. Tyler still calls her his favorite teacher.

Our dear friends Keith and MaryAnn Smith, and their children (Meredith, Shannon, and Jason), who always supported us and made Tyler feel as comfortable in their home as he is in ours. Our friends at the Knights of Columbus Edward Douglas White Council, where Tyler landed his first job and where I know he will always have a family. Pride and self-motivation seemed foreign to Tyler until last summer, the summer before his 18th birthday, when he worked as a counselor at the Knights' day camp. "I have a job," Tyler beamed one day. "Can you believe I have a job?" Yes, we can.

Dr. Catherine McCarthy, a smart and compassionate resource who helped Lori create a support system for Tyler. Jean Gold, who gave Lori somebody better than her husband to talk through life's challenges.

The friends and associates who critiqued manuscript drafts, including Frank Bruni, Matthew Dowd, Mark Leibovich, David Maraniss, Olivia Morgan, Joe Scarborough, Mindy Tucker Fletcher, Stephen Gray Wallace, and Patsy Wilson. Close friend and former Associated Press colleague Ted Anthony, who was my brainstormer-in-chief from the first paragraph of *First, Family* to the last gasp of *Love That Boy*.

Adam Kushner, the *National Journal* editor (he's now with the *Washington Post*), who rejected my first submission of *First, Family* because I had written it as a political analysis. He was intrigued by a quote from Tyler that I had buried in the story: "I hope I don't let you down, Dad." Adam asked me, "How did it make you feel when Tyler said that to you?" I shrugged. "When your son basically said he was afraid to embarrass you," Adam repeated. "How did that make you *feel?*" He forced me to write about my feelings, the hardest assignment of my career.

My book agent, Andrew Stuart, and the mutual friend who brought us together, Carl Cannon.

Rick Horgan, my first editor at Crown. He forced me outside my comfort zone. Rejecting the first 30,000-word submission, Rick emailed, "You are not writing the book I want, and I am guessing that your confusion about what the book is has made the process of writing agonizing." He was right.

Heather Jackson took over from Rick and found the joy in it. "None of us owns your brain, heart, ideas, experience," she emailed me after inheriting the book. "We can ultimately only try to help you best shepherd those." Heather is a brilliant and caring partner who, more than anybody other than Lori, deserves credit for getting this done.

My friends, colleagues, and supervisors at Atlantic Media, including Tim Grieve, Bruce Gottlieb, Tim Hartman, Andy Sareyan, and Justin Smith. The owner of the enterprise, David Bradley, expects two qualities in his employees: "extreme excellence" and a "spirit of generosity." I benefited from both.

David recruited me from the Associated Press about the same time Tyler was diagnosed with Asperger's syndrome, promising us the flexibility to both manage the autism and complete Lori's newly hatched father-son project. Over dinner at his home with wife, Katherine, David told Lori and me, "Tyler is now part of our family." The Bradleys never wavered.

Scott Willyerd and his team at Dick Jones Communications, who wrangled experts on parenting and child development to start my reporting. Gina Ranfone and Jordan Bloom, who conducted research on child-rearing for me in the summer and fall of 2013.

The staff at the library near our tiny northern Michigan town, who provided a home away from home. Rob Malan, who built us a sanctuary in the woods there for me to work on this book and, perhaps, write my next.

I write these last words while thumbing through a six-inch stack of emails from people who read the *National Journal* essay. They inspired me. I replied to every email. Some readers wrote back—and many were among the more than three dozen mothers, fathers, and adult children I interviewed for this book. Some asked me to shield their identities.

Every mother and father asks themselves, "How can I be a better parent?"

The best answer may have come from the cable news intern who is now a rising Democratic operative with many friends (including me) and a proud mother and father. "My parents had big expectations for me," he told me several months after our awkward introduction. "They wanted me to be what I wanted to become."

BIBLIOGRAPHY

Abboud, Soo Kim. *Top of the Class*. Berkley Publishing Group, New York, 2005.

Attwood, Tony. *The Complete Guide to Asperger's Syndrome*. Jessica Kingsley Publishers, London, 2007.

Bishop, Joseph Bucklin, ed. *Theodore Roosevelt's Letters to His Children*. Charles Scribner's Sons, New York, 1919.

Boyd, Brenda. *Parenting a Child with Asperger Syndrome*. Jessica Kingsley Publishers, London, 2003.

Bruni, Frank. *Where You Go Is Not Who You'll Be: An Antidote to the College Admissions Mania*. Hachette Book Group, New York, 2015.

Caffrey, Janine Walker. *Drive: Advice from Middle School to College and Beyond*. Da Capo Press, Philadelphia, 2008.

Cillessen, Antonius H. N., David Schwartz, and Lara Mayeux. *Popularity in the Peer System*. Guilford Press, New York, 2011.

Finch, David. *The Journal of Best Practices: Memoir of Marriage, Asperger Syndrome, and One Man's Quest to Be a Better Husband*. Scribner, New York, 2012.

Gaffigan, Jim. *Dad Is Fat*. Random House, New York, 2013.

Grandin, Temple. *Thinking in Pictures: My Life with Autism.* Random House, New York, 1995.

Grandin, Temple. *The Way I See It.* Future Horizons, Arlington, TX, 2011.

Grandin, Temple, and Richard Panek. *The Autistic Brain.* Houghton Mifflin Harcourt Publishing, New York, 2013.

Hallowell, Edward M. *The Childhood Roots of Adult Happiness.* Random House, New York, 2002.

Hicks, Marybeth. *Bringing Up Geeks: Genuine, Enthusiastic, Empowered Kids.* Penguin Publishing Group, New York, 2008.

Honoré, Carl. *Under Pressure.* HarperCollins, New York, 2008.

Huffington, Arianna. *Thrive.* Random House, New York, 2015.

Hulbert, Ann. *Raising America.* Random House, New York, 2003.

Kimmel, Tim. *Raising Kids for True Greatness.* Thomas Nelson, Nashville, TN, 2006.

Kindlow, Dan, and Michael Thompson. *Raising Cain: Protecting the Emotional Life of Boys.* Random House, New York, 1999.

Levine, Madeline. *The Price of Privilege.* HarperCollins, New York, 2006.

Levine, Madeline. *Teach Your Children Well.* HarperCollins, New York, 2012.

Palmiter, David J., Jr. *Working Parents, Thriving Families: 10 Strategies That Make a Difference.* Sunrise River Press, North Branch, MN, 2011.

Payne, Kim John. *Simplicity Parenting.* Random House, New York, 2009.

Pope, Denise, Maureen Brown, and Sarah Miles. *Overloaded and Underprepared.* Jossey-Bass, San Francisco, 2015.

Robison, John Elder. *Look Me in the Eye: My Life with Asperger's*. Random House, New York, 2008.

Robison, John Elder. *Raising Cubby: A Father and Son's Adventures with Asperger's, Trains, Tractors, and High Explosives*. Random House, New York, 2013.

Rosenfeld, Alvin, and Nicole Wise. *The Over-Scheduled Child: Avoiding the Hyper-Parenting Trap*. St. Martin's Press, New York, 2000.

Senior, Jennifer. *All Joy and No Fun: The Paradox of Modern Parenthood*. HarperCollins, New York, 2014.

Silberman, Steve. *NeuroTribes: The Legacy of Autism and the Future of Neurodiversity*. Penguin Group, New York, 2015.

Solomon, Andrew. *Far from the Tree: Parents, Children, and the Search for Identity*. Simon & Schuster, New York, 2012.

Sommers, Christina Hoff. *The War Against Boys*. Simon & Schuster, New York, 2000.

Stearns, Peter. *Anxious Parents*. New York University Press, New York, 2003.

Taylor, Jim. *Positive Pushing: How to Raise a Successful and Happy Child*. Hyperion, New York, 2002.

Wallace, Stephen Gray. *Reality Gap: Alcohol, Drugs, and Sex— What Parents Don't Know and Teens Aren't Telling*. Sterling, New York, 2008.

Wead, Doug. *All the President's Children*. Atria Books, New York, 2003.

Willey, Liane Holliday. *Asperger's Syndrome in the Family*. Jessica Kingsley Publishers, London, 2001.

INDEX

LOVE THAT BOY

A Reader's Guide

1. In the doctor's office immediately prior to hearing Tyler's autism diagnosis, Ron and Lori are holding hands. Ron notices an unfinished puzzle on the floor next to a worn wooden train with its locomotive missing. A puzzle piece has long been an emblem of the autism community. Must a child be autistic to be an "unfinished puzzle," or does that symbol apply to all children? As a mother or father, do you ever feel like a powerless locomotive? If so, when? What can you do about it?

2. At the end of the introduction, Ron refers to the toy train and a single puzzle piece as "misfits of a tidy office." Do all children, at some point, feel like misfits, or just those on the autism spectrum? What is the real-life analogue to "a tidy office"?

3. On the first "guilt trip," Tyler is practicing his handshakes just before meeting President Obama and tells his father, "I hope I don't let you down, Dad." How do you think Ron felt hearing that? How would it make you feel to hear it

from one of your children? Do you ever put too much pressure on your kids?

4. After the Obama meeting, Ron says he realizes the problem isn't Tyler or even autism. "It's me." What does he mean by that?

5. Do you agree with Ron that childhood popularity is a "trap"? Why or why not?

6. When Tyler says he is "my kind of happy," what does he mean? Do you think there's a gap between your idea of happiness and your child's?

7. At the end of "Grit," Ron notices President Clinton missing subtle social clues and wonders if perhaps we're all on the autism spectrum. Do you think he meant that literally or was he making a broader point?

8. Were you surprised that President George W. Bush's chapter was titled "Empathy"? After all, it was President Clinton who famously told voters, "I feel your pain," and whose greatest political gift is thought to be empathy. Is there a difference between connecting with a crowd and connecting with a person? Why do you think Bush connected with Tyler better than his own father? Have you ever noticed somebody other than you relating to your child better than you? How did that make you feel?

9. Ron posits that human decency motivated the ex-presidents to meet with his young Aspie. Why do you think they cooperated? Do you agree they are "fundamentally good people in a bad system"? What, if anything, did you learn anew about Clinton and Bush by reading *Love That Boy?*

10. It's easy to criticize parents for their excessive expectations. But aren't there good reasons for pressuring our children to do better and be better? What are those reasons? How does a parent learn to recognize the difference between pushing and guiding?

11. The chapter on happiness ends with a scene in which Ron's father is so exhausted from Holly's wedding that he cannot close his own zipper, and yet he gets out of the car for a family photo. Ron wrote of his dad, "He was still The Guy, full of goodness." What does that scene tell you about the true meaning of happiness? How might you pursue happiness differently?

12. On page ninety-six, Ron tells parents to "just chill" and concludes a section on the superstar syndrome by writing, "We should refashion parenthood by tolerating pain, play, and failure." Do you agree? How might you apply it to your family?

13. Were you surprised at the end of the book to see Tyler step forward to comfort his grandmother when his father and uncles could not? What did that scene say about his development? What does it say about the potential of all children to exceed their parents' expectations? If you are a parent, do your kids ever exceed yours?

14. *Love That Boy* ends with this passage: "Now, finally, I know what perfect is. It's a child blessed with the grace to show goodness, even on the worst of days. No, Tyler is not my idealized son. He is my ideal one." Think about your own family. How does your child meet this definition of perfect? How are you still striving to be perfect? And what is the difference between our idealized and ideal selves?

ABOUT THE AUTHOR

RON FOURNIER is the publisher and editor of Crain's Detroit Business and an award-winning and nationally acclaimed political contributor to *The Atlantic*. He began his family and career in Arkansas, covering then governor Bill Clinton before moving to Washington in 1993, where he reported on politics and the presidency during the administrations of Clinton, George W. Bush, and Barack Obama. Fournier also served as a fellow at the Harvard Institute of Politics, where he cowrote the *New York Times* bestseller *Applebee's America*. He holds the Society of Professional Journalists' Sigma Delta Chi Award for coverage of the 2000 elections, and he is a four-time winner of the prestigious White House Correspondents' Association Merriman Smith Memorial Award.